Bichon Frise
Handbook

Richard G. Beauchamp

Filled with Full-color Photographs
Illustrations by Michele Earle-Bridges

About the Author

Richard G. (Rick) Beauchamp has been actively involved with the Bichon Frise breed since its earliest days in America. He has bred over seventy champions in the breed, among them many Best In Show and Variety Group winners. He owned Ch. Chaminade Mr. Beau Monde, the top producing sire in the breed (65 champions) and bred Ch. Beau Monde The Fire Cracker, top producing dam in the breed (17 champions). He participated in writing the American Kennel Club standard for the breed. Rick is an AKC judge and has judged purebred dogs in every major country of the world along with lecturing and writing about dogs of all breeds. He judged Bichon Frises at the 2004 Crufts show in England—the world's largest dog show.

Photo Credits

Kent and Donna Dannen, 8, 11, 16, 19, 21, 25, 53, 67, 70, 71, 72, 77, 80, 82, 92, 95, 105, 113, 116, 134, 147 (both photos); Jean M. Fogle, 88, 100 (both photos), 102; Chris Lynch, 42 (upper left); Pets by Paulette, vii, 6, 12, 17, 24, 31, 33, 40, 48, 54, 74, 110, 133, 142, 145 (bottom); Connie Summers, 9, 10, 84, 99, 143, 145 (top); Chuck Tatham, 5; Toni Tucker, 3, 14, 18, 57 (both photos); 58 (bottom), 59 (both photos), 60, 61, 62 (three photos), 63, 64, (four photos), 65 (five photos), 66 (three photos), 69, 136, 139; Missy Yuhl, 42 (lower left).

Acknowledgments

The Bichon Frise has been a part of my life for well over 30 years. So often over those years I've thought of one thing or another about the breed that someone should write about for new owners. Had it not been for the enthusiastic support at Barron's Educational Series I would probably still be thinking about all those things. However, with the staff's encouragement all those important facts (and more!) became *The Bichon Frise Handbook*. I feel certain the readers of this book will find a great deal within its pages to help make living with a Bichon a joyful, long-term relationship for both dog and owner.

I particularly want to thank my editor, Seymour Weiss, who assisted me so well in consolidating all the bits and pieces of my experiences with Bichons into this book. He smoothed out a good number of rocky turns along the way.

Most of all a special thank you to "Christopher" (Ch. Chaminade Mr. Beau Monde), my own first Bichon whose excellence inspired a lifetime of admiration for the breed.

Cover Photos

Front cover: Pets by Paulette, top and bottom right; Toni Tucker, left, center left and bottom left; Back cover and inside front cover: Pets by Paulette. Inside back cover: Toni Tucker.

© Copyright 2005 by Barron's Educational Series, Inc. All rights reserved. No part of this book may be reproduced in any form, by photostat, microfilm, xerography, or any other means, or incorporated into any information retrieval system, electronic or mechanical, without the written permission of the copyright owner.

All inquiries should be addressed to:
Barron's Educational Series, Inc.
250 Wireless Boulevard
Hauppauge, New York 11788
www.barronseduc.com

International Standard Book No. 0-7641-2782-9

Library of Congress Catalog Card No. 2004047657

Library of Congress Cataloging-in-Publication Data
Beauchamp, Richard G.
  The Bichon frise handbook / Richard G. Beauchamp.
    p. cm.
  Includes bibliographical references and index.
  ISBN 0-7641-2782-9
  1. Bichon frise. I. Title.

SF429.B52B432 2004
636.72—dc22   2004047657

Printed in China
9 8 7 6 5 4 3 2 1

This pet handbook gives advice to the reader about buying and caring for a new dog. The author and publisher consider it important to point out that the advice given in the book applies to normally developed puppies or adult dogs, obtained from recognized dog breeders or adoption shelters—dogs that have been examined and are in excellent health with good temperament.

Anyone who adopts a grown dog should be aware that the animal has already formed its basic impression of human beings and their customs. The new owner should watch the animal carefully, especially its attitude toward humans. If possible, the new owner should meet the former owner before adopting the dog. If the dog is adopted from a shelter, the new owner should make an effort to obtain information about the dog's background, personality, and peculiarities. Dogs that come from abusive homes or from homes in which they have been treated abnormally may react to handling in an unnatural manner, and may have a tendency to snap or bite. Dogs with this nature should only be adopted by people who have had experience with such dogs.

Caution is further advised in the association of children with dogs, both puppies and adults, and in meeting other dogs, whether on or off lead.

Well-behaved and carefully supervised dogs may cause damage to someone else's property or cause accidents. It is therefore in the owner's interest to be adequately insured against such eventualities, and we strongly urge all dog owners to purchase liability policies that cover their dogs.

Contents

Preface

Most books written about an individual dog breed do their utmost to convince the reader that the breed at hand is not only perfect in every respect but also is the ideal companion for every one who has ever considered owning a dog. *The Bichon Frise Handbook* most definitely does not fit this mold.

The only people I want to even consider inviting a Bichon Frise (pronounced Bee-*shawn* Free-*zay*) into their home are those who are willing to put up with all the work involved. Bichons should only live with dog lovers who are aware that dogs are not "little people" and have very special needs and distinct ways of learning family rules.

Bichons, without a doubt, are one of the most delightful breeds known to man—a joy to live with. That is, *if and only if,* their owners have the time and patience to allow the breed's effervescent nature to grow and develop.

Along with all the wonderful qualities I have attributed to the Bichon, there are a few drawbacks. Life is just a bowl of cherries to the average Bichon, and the rules and regulations that apply to most dogs are seen as a bother to this fun-loving breed. It sometimes takes determination to get a Bichon to concentrate on the fact that there is a time to learn and a time to play.

If you are or have decided to become a Bichon owner and are willing to support your dog in becoming the wonderful little companion the breed can be, your choice has been a good one. The two of you will have many fun filled adventures in the years to come.

The well-bred Bichon Frise has all the potential in the world of being a joyful and loving companion but it takes the time and patience of a caring owner to allow that delightful personality to grow and develop.

Chapter One

From Whence They Came

History of the Bichon Frise

The beguiling personality and teddy bear attractiveness of the Bichon Frise can distract those who are attracted to the breed from a very important fact. The Bichon Frise is a *dog* and though it has taken thousands of years, this breed like all breeds of dogs traces its development to the same common ancestor. Because of their like heritage Bichons have many of the same canine needs as their countless cousins. Their canine relatives may be larger or more aggressive, but in the end, Bichons are simply *dogs.*

All dogs, from the tiniest toy breed to the most massive of the working breeds have one common ancestor—the wolf. How the wolf evolved into man's best friend is as fascinating as it is ancient. It began over ten thousand years ago in the dawning of the Mesolithic period.

The Bichon Frise breed traveled the world many times over on his journey to become one of America's most appealing household companions.

The more human-friendly from the wolf packs were most apt to have been granted access to human campsites. In turn, the cubs of those more privileged wolves were raised in proximity to humans. This took the wolves further along the path to domestication.

It was found certain descendants of these steadily more domesticated wolves were able to assist in a number of early human survival pursuits. An ability to bring down the fleet of foot game that roamed the land was particularly useful and earned the wolf an even more important place in human life.

Closer association was to reveal the wolf's wider capabilities. Soon these evolving wolves were sounding the alarm when intruders approached, hauling heavy loads, going to earth after game and eventually even assisting in the retrieving of wounded game on both land and water. Slowly, over many centuries, the wolf, *Canis Lupus,* became a very different animal—what we know today as the dog, *Canis Familiaris.*

Documentation of controlled breeding can be found as early as the

1

first century A.D. when the Romans classified dogs into general groups: guard dogs, shepherd's dogs, fighting or war dogs, and hunting dogs. The hunting dogs were designated as those that hunted by sight and others that hunted by scent.

Many breeds can be traced directly to members of these early groups. Combining individuals from two or more of these categories developed other breeds.

The combination of interest here created the Bichon family. This new family was the result of combining the blood of a medium-sized water spaniel type dog and a simultaneously existing family of light-colored small "lap" or ladies' dogs that are said to have had their origin in the Far East.

The water spaniels were known as the Barbet. From this combination a small, often white breed of dog evolved that was known as the "small Barbet" or Barbichon (later shortened to Bichon). These little white dogs were known to have existed throughout the area surrounding the Mediterranean Sea before the time of Christ. The combination that produced the Barbichon also proved to be the basis for a number of other small "companion" breeds, not the least of which were the breeds known today as the Maltese and the Poodle.

As urbanization occurred, smaller dogs became very popular. Instead of being companions of only the hunting members of the family, the smaller dogs moved indoors and became members of the immediate household, women and children included.

The Bichon "Varieties" Develop

Because they were small enough, these companion dogs often traveled with their owners, some of whom were seamen who fancied the Bichon's small-size hardiness and amiable dispositions and took the little dogs along as reminders of home.

It is said that these sailors quickly found that their little Bichons not only had value as trade, but also had great appeal among the ladies in foreign ports. Before long, young ladies in lands as far off as the Philippines, Cuba, Argentina, and Tenerife were waving good-bye to their seafaring lovers, tears in eyes and Bichons in arms.

These little dogs flourished in their new homes, developing into several distinct varieties. These were to become known as the Bichon Maltaise, the Bichon Bolognese, the Bichon Havanese and the Bichon Tenerife. The Bichon Tenerife is chiefly credited as the forerunner of today's Bichon Frise. However, the similar origin of all Bichons, their subsequent interrelated histories, and their physical similarities cast doubt on crediting the dog from Tenerife as the Bichon Frise's only ancestor. Problems of modern breeders in maintaining the desired "look" constantly recall obvious characteristics of their close relatives.

Bichon Frise (nee Tenerife)

The Canary and Tenerife Islands are considered the developmental centers of the breed that was known for many years as the Bichon Tenerife and later as the Bichon Frise.

It can only be assumed the indigenous breeds of the new lands crossed with the Bichon type dogs left behind by travelers. These crosses obviously flourished and generations later their descendants made their way full circle back to both Spain and Italy.

During the 1500s, highly influenced by Italy's Renaissance, it was very fashionable in France to adopt everything Italian. Part of the fashion trend in the French courts was Italy's little white Bichon Tenerife. Francis I, patron of the Renaissance, was particularly fond of the breed during his reign (1515–1547 A.D.) .

After that period little appears in French literature about the Tenerife dog until the rise of Napoleon III in the early years of the nineteenth century. The Bichon Tenerife is frequently mentioned in French literature during that century and is frequently portrayed with members of the royal courts by leading artists of the period.

By the end of the nineteenth century the breed was replaced in the favor of the court, but hardy breed that it was the Bichon Tenerife survived and was often found in the streets of Paris and other cities accompanying tradesmen and street

As hard as it is to imagine, our friendly Bichon Frise, like all other breeds of dog, traces its development back thousands of years to the same common ancestor— the wolf.

musicians. The nimble Bichons were highly trainable and loved to perform. The breed demonstrated a unique ability to walk on its hind legs for long distances and usually did so while pawing the air. Interpreting this as begging for money, passersby good-humoredly responded.

Europe's great circuses and carnivals took advantage of the Bichon's extroverted personality and uncanny ability to learn and perform tricks. The dogs were undoubtedly bred and the offspring selected for the ability to entertain. To this day the breed retains this capability, and Bichon owners are amazed to find their dogs walking on their hind legs, performing somersaults, and performing feats of dexterity with no training whatsoever.

A good deal of controversy surrounds the when and where of the name "Bichon Frise," but we do know that the *Encyclopedia of Dogs* (Thomas Y. Crowell Co., New York), produced under direction of The Federation Cynologique Internationale (FCI), gives the Bichon Frise's country of origin as France. The FCI has given itself the responsibility of deciding all things canine throughout Europe.

Were it not for the indestructible constitution of the Bichon, however, the breed could well have been lost during the First and Second World Wars. Reduced to minimal numbers by the end of World War I, the breed escaped extinction only through the efforts of a few valiant fanciers who gathered what remained of the breed from the streets of France and Belgium. Working cooperatively, those who found pleasure in the happy little dogs obtained breed recognition under the auspices of the Societé Centrale Canine in March 1933. The breed was officially given the name "the Bichon A Poil Frisé" — "the Bichon of the curly hair."

Just when it looked as though devotees had secured the future of the Bichon Frise, another Great War threatened the newly named breed. Here again the breed's hardiness and the determination of its owners assisted the Bichon Frise through this next devastating ordeal.

There can be little doubt that the checkered history of the Bichon Frise through the centuries included liaisons with its three cousins. The breed was classified and legitimized as a pure and distinct breed by the French in 1933. However, what remained of the breed in Europe after the close of World War II was most likely a conglomerate of the Bichon varieties.

This, combined with the practice at the time in some European countries of permitting dogs of unknown parentage to be registered and used as breeding stock saved the Bichon Frise from total extinction. On the other hand it would prove to severely complicate the task of setting a distinct type. There is documented evidence that accepting dogs of unknown parentage into the Bichon registries of some European countries existed at least until the early 1970s.

Across the Pond

In 1952, an important year for the Bichon Frise, Helene and Francois Picault of Dieppe, France became interested in the breed. They exhibited briefly in France and eventually immigrated to America, where they optimistically anticipated making a fortune by selling their little white dogs.

As is usual with dogs, the anticipated "fortune" never was to come for the Picaults. Their family of Bichons grew rapidly while sales for animals not registered with the AKC were hard to come by regardless of

History Makers

The first Bichon Frise to complete its American championship was Charles and Dolores Wolskie's C & D Count Kristopher.

The first all breed Best In Show to be won by a Bichon was at Farmington Valley Kennel Club on July 7, 1973. Mr. Louis Murr selected Mrs. William Tabler's Ch. Chaminade Syncopation for the award, just three short months after the breed had gained AKC recognition. The handler was Ted Young, Jr.

The first winner of the Bichon Frise Club of America's National Specialty show was Mrs. Nan Busk's Ch. Vogelflight's Music Man. Judge Mr. Langdon Skarda made the award, in June 1976. Handler was Joe Waterman.

The first Bichon to win Best In Show all Breeds at Westminster Kennel Club was Ch. Special Times Just Right. Owners: Cecelia Ruggles, Eleanor McDonald, and Flavio Werneck. The date was February 14, 2001. The Judge was Dorothy M. Macdonald. The handler was Scott Sommer.

Almost every dog fancier dreams of a Westminster Best in Show win. For "J.R," Ch. Special Times Just Right, his breeder, his owners, and his handler, their historic Valentine's Day 2001 Garden triumph was indeed a special time that was just right!

The two World Wars had a devastating effect on the Bichon Frise. The breed was saved from extinction, however, by the determined efforts of fanciers who refused to allow their favorite to disappear into oblivion.

the breed's charm. During 1960 and 1961 a few breeders acquired stock from the Picaults and a few others imported stock from France and Belgium.

In 1961, the Picaults were at the end of their patience and finances when, as fate would have it, they met Gertrude Fournier of San Diego, California. Enchanted with the breed, she felt sure she could assist them in securing publicity and eventual recognition for the white charmers. Mrs. Fournier had gained some note as a Collie breeder under the Cali-Col prefix, but to signify a new partnership with the Picaults the name Pic-Four betokened the surnames of both interested parties.

But fame and recognition continued to elude the breed and the Picaults were again denied their dreamed-of fortune. The limits of the partnership created discontent for both parties and through a series of events Mrs. Fournier became sole owner of all the dogs.

Hitting the "Big Time"

As a result of the breed's devoted followers the AKC accepted the Bichon Frise into Miscellaneous Class competition in September, 1971. This class was and still is the first step a new breed takes on its way to full recognition by the AKC.

In the following two years the breed attracted greater attention and had such universal acceptance by dog fanciers it was hard to believe it was not a fully accredited AKC breed. Then the really good news! Late in 1972 it was announced the Bichon Frise had been granted full recognition by the AKC.

On April 8, 1973, Mrs. Winifred Heckmann judged the Silver State Kennel Club in Las Vegas, Nevada, the first show at which the Bichon Frise was eligible to receive championship points. Her selection for Winners Dog, Best of Winners and Best of Breed was Mrs. Gertrude Fournier's Cali-Col's Scalawag; Winners Bitch, Best Opposite Sex was Teena Sarkissian's Chaminade Phoenicia. Scalawag then went on to place second in the Non-Sporting Group under Mr. John Cramer.

Chapter Two
Look Before You Leap

The Inside Scoop

In most cases Bichons will get along with anyone willing to get along with them. They are more than happy to do so in a Manhattan apartment or down on an Iowa farm. I know Bichons who live in both places and they adjust to city life as easily as living in the country. Bichons do fit in just about anywhere because they are small enough not to need a Land Rover to be hauled around in, yet big enough not to be blown two counties away by the first brisk wind.

Note, however, that as greeting-card appealing a Bichon puppy might be, this is a *white* dog that needs frequent bathing to stay white. To make matters worse, the Bichon is the eternal child and enjoys playing in the mud or the sandbox as much as any human child.

The Bichon is a long-coated breed that will stay looking like a Bichon only in-so-long as you keep your dog brushed. You must either learn the routine or be willing to pay for professional grooming. If you appreciate the look of the breed, understand that it will take time and effort to keep your Bichon looking that way.

Neglect of a Bichon's coat insures matting that attracts debris and parasites. Quicker than you might guess it will be necessary to have the neglected Bichon shaved to the skin. The average person doesn't realize that the coats of the long-haired breeds serve as insulation against both heat and cold. Shaving your Bichon isn't doing her a favor; it is making her even more uncomfortable than carrying around that felted coat. I can't help but wonder why the person who neglects, then shaves his coated dog doesn't get a smooth-coated breed in the first place.

If you are willing to make the commitment that a Bichon requires there are few breeds more versatile, amiable, or adaptable. Bichons have been pampered pets of the nobility, seafarers, street urchins, and circus entertainers. With a history like that the Bichon can fit into almost any caring and compatible household— in town or country.

A well-bred Bichon Frise can be just as happy and well adjusted living in a Manhattan apartment as she would be down on the farm.

A Bichon can give her owner unfailing cheerfulness and devotion and, surprising as it may sound, the Bichon can also make a very good little watchdog. Don't expect little "Ami" to tackle an intruder or hold him at bay, but sound the alarm she will! The police will vouch that the mere existence of a dog in the home is nearly as great a robbery deterrent as a complex and expensive security system.

The Bichon's early warning of an intruder will give you time to dial 911. The dog's not to be missed warning bark will deter the average intruder, who is never sure if that is a little bark of a big dog or a big bark of a little dog. Most would-be thieves are not willing to risk being wrong in this respect.

You can rely upon your Bichon to let you know the doorbell has rung or someone is knocking at the door. But constant and needless barking will not disturb you. All that said, once *you* let a stranger in, forget further protection. Bichons love company!

Bichons love well-mannered children and can enjoy playing catch with Junior as much as a tea party with Mary Jane. The breed is neither too rough for the timid nor too timid for the active youngsters.

Personality Plus

As stated, throughout its history the Bichon has been a close companion to people. Whether darling of royal courts or circus performer, everything the Bichon has done has been in the company of humans. A Bichon is happiest when allowed to continue that association. The would-be buyer must understand that this is not a breed to be shut away in a kennel or outdoor run with only occasional access to its owner's environment.

That simply will not work. If your lifestyle doesn't accommodate the in-home companionship of a dog, you would be far better served by another breed. The very essence of the Bichon is in its sparkling personality and sensitive nature. The only way it can be fully developed is by constant human contact.

The Bichon is not a vindictive breed, but it doesn't surprise me to hear that a completely housebroken

Bichon will abruptly forget training in protest of suddenly being left alone too often or too long. Some Bichons will let you know they are not getting the attention they need by destroying household items. Invariably they'll choose a personal item belonging to their owner or a family member they are particularly fond of. I think it's done less out of spite than in an attempt to ingest the essence of the person whose attention the dog craves.

Home Alone

None of this should be construed that only those who are home all day to cater to their dog can be a Bichon owner. We know many working people who are away most of the day whose Bichons are well-mannered when left home alone. The key seems to be *quality* rather than *quantity* of time spent with their pet. Morning or evening walks, grooming sessions, game time, and simply having your Bichon share your life when you are home is vital to the breed's personality development and attitude. Bichons like to be talked to and praised. The adage, "No man is an island" needs to be expanded to include dogs—especially Bichons.

Everything about the Bichon's personality indicates it is a nonaggressive breed. Generally the breed is submissive. We have never seen a Bichon challenge her owner regardless of how much she might object to what she is being asked to do. A stern tone is usually more than sufficient to let your Bichon know your disapproval. It is never necessary to strike a Bichon. A sharp "No!" is normally more than enough.

Because of the breed's easygoing nature, the Bichon is content to remain at home with her family and is not prone to wander. Since the Bichon is a lover of *all* humans she is not beyond accepting a ride in an automobile or an invitation to play, even if the invitation is from a total stranger. Secure fences and closely latched doors and gates preclude that happening.

A Bichon will only look like the breed that caught your eye as long as you are willing to keep your dog brushed and trimmed. You must either learn the routine yourself or pay a professional to do that all-important work on a regular basis.

Bichons love well-mannered children, and are just as happy playing games with the boys as they are having tea parties with the girls.

Easy Does It

The Bichon makes a great effort to please her owner and is highly trainable as long as the trainer is not heavy-handed. Training problems are far more apt to be due to the owner rather than a Bichon's lack of understanding or inability to learn.

Setting boundaries is as important to your Bichon's well-being as it is to your relationship with her. The sooner she understands there are rules to be obeyed the easier it will be for her to become an enjoyable companion. The time it takes for you to establish those rules will deter-

mine how quickly this will come about. As noted, the Bichon is not vindictive or particularly stubborn, but she needs your guidance to understand the parameters within which she can operate.

How About You?

The foregoing gives you an idea of life with the average Bichon. Will all Bichons act and react in that exact manner? Probably not, but close. We're dealing with living creatures that react to influences individually. What may affect "puppy A" might not even phase "puppy B." But by and large, Bichons are easy to get along with as long as they are given ample opportunity to be with "their people."

A well-bred and well-trained Bichon has qualities that have made the breed an ideal family dog. You must understand, however, that the operative words are "well-bred and well-trained." Too many would-be Bichon owners fulfill their dreams of Bichon ownership by rushing to the local mall and buying the first puppy advertised as "100 percent pedigreed pure Bichon." They don't consider the temperament and constitution of the parents or the work involved in creating a good canine citizen out of that curly mop of raw material.

Before dashing out to buy one of these fluff balls, there are a number of important things you need to do. First, think of your experience with pets of any kind. Was feeding the goldfish such a chore you had to call in assistance from Fish Aid? Did refilling the bird feeder get done only once the whole winter?

Think very clearly about your lifestyle or that of your family. You may be single and a workaholic who is home long enough only to change clothes before heading back to the office. Your family may be involved in so many activities that coming and going extends around the clock.

None of these scenarios is conducive to raising and training a Bichon puppy. The puppy that you bring into your home has no knowledge of household rules nor the ability to fend for itself while you or the family are elsewhere.

Once a dog enters your household it will be there all day, every day. It will rely entirely upon you for care and comfort. If getting a dog was your idea, don't rely upon others in the family to help unless they have already volunteered to do so.

Kids in the family may be ready to *promise* that "Fluff" will be their first priority. Don't depend on it. A child's first priority can mean one thing today and something else tomorrow. Do not use a living creature to test your children's level of responsibility! There are other means of teaching responsibility without a helpless animal suffering a child's failure.

If you enter your commitment understanding that in some respects pets are more work than children, you'll do well! Your dog can't grab a snack out of the refrigerator when it is hungry. It has no desire to be toilet trained and could not care less

The Bichon is an extremely versatile breed that enjoys quiet times at home as well as adventure trips outdoors.

about cleaning up its own mess. Nor is it going to take dance classes or join the soccer team to drain that energy level.

All that is up to you, you and only you! If you plan to hire someone to take care of those things for you just so you can relax and have some ears to scratch, save yourself the time, burden, and money; get a stuffed toy or pet rock.

If growing a few African violets or giving a plant an occasional drink of

Don't have unrealistic expectations of your dog. Your Bichon puppy will arrive with a blank slate. What will appear on that slate is what *you* or what the puppy will express. Make sure what appears on that slate is what you want to be there.

Your Bichon puppy will arrive in your home with a blank slate. What will appear on that slate determines what kind of a companion she will be.

water proved to be drudgery, dog care is going to make you feel like an indentured servant! Potted plants shrivel after a few weeks of neglect. When a Bichon is neglected she will eat your shoes and wet on the carpet. She doesn't do this out of spite; it's her way out of boredom and proves lack of supervision.

In nature, when wolf cubs begin to venture from the nest their mother made for them, they look for two important things—a pack leader and the pack rules that let them know what they may and may not do. Surprisingly, despite human meddling in the transition of wolf to domesticated dog, the canine world's needs remain much the same.

Just like his distant ancestor, a Bichon looks for a leader and wants to know the pack's rules. Since your pup does not reside in the North Woods, guess who is to perform the duties of the pack leader? If you guess yourself, you are on track.

If you provide what your puppy needs, you will have a great companion. If you don't, you will have headaches!

Swingin' Singles

If you live alone, ownership is simple on one hand, complicated on the other; you will be sole caregiver. But if you do live alone, you probably have to leave for work each day to keep little Ami in dog biscuits. Who then, will sit and hold your little white whirlwind's busy little paw?

Leaving this bundle of curiosity alone with the run of the house all day will do nothing for her personality and less for your household goods. A very young Bichon left alone day after day will lack the thing it needs most—human companionship. Bichons are people dogs and need one-on-one attention. Unless you plan to compensate for your time away your Bichon will not be a happy camper.

If you do live alone you will need to make the necessary commitment dog ownership entails. That includes someone to look in on the little angel when she is just a puppy.

If you share your life with a significant other or an entire family, the needs of others will have to be considered. Your significant other may not be interested in your twosome becoming a threesome.

In many households mothers, even working mothers, win the drawing for "Who'll-take-care-of-Ami-when-the-family's-away?" We know that mothers are modern day Wonder Women, but all too often they're saddled with the responsibility of caring for the dog they really didn't want in the first place. The lady of your household might not be as keen as you are about adopting another needy child. Remember— *this was your idea!*

Don't forget about training. Bichons need a lot of it as youngsters. Training takes time and patience (with a strong emphasis on the latter). This should take place daily, whether it happens before work, after work, or on the lunch break. It has to happen. Not feeling up to it doesn't count. Not only must you feel up to it, you must *be* up to it. Your state of mind will have a great deal to do with how well your training sessions go.

Losing patience and taking it out on your Bichon doesn't work. Bichons are extremely sensitive. Yell a little too loud at a Bichon and you'll see what I mean. A properly raised Bichon understands and accepts correction, but the breed does not tolerate abuse. If subjected to continuous abusive treatment even the best temperament will be destroyed.

This doesn't mean a Bichon can't be corrected. On the contrary, a Bichon puppy has to start learning household rules from the first day she comes to your home. If the puppy is to believe you and learn to avoid certain behavior, the *"No!"* command has to mean no all the time—not just most of the time or when she decides she wants to respond.

Bichons are comfort creatures. They will find the softest spot in the house on which to lounge unless otherwise instructed. The sofa will never be a forbidden zone for your Bichon if you relent and allow her to jump up and cuddle with you on those rainy days when you're feeling in need of comfort. Bichons have difficulty relating to the very human concepts of "some time" and "changing minds."

Rule enforcement is one of the important reasons to have a place to stash Ami when you are too busy to insist rules be obeyed. A securely fenced yard, a fenced and gated outdoor run, or a fiberglass shipping kennel for indoors will keep your Bichon contained and out of mischief when you are involved in activities that would keep your attention elsewhere.

It is very important that the puppy you select comes from a breeding program that has been carefully selected for longevity, and is as free of genetic problems as possible.

A Little Road Work

For your Bichon to develop properly both mentally and physically she'll need plenty of exercise. Young puppies usually get enough with those sudden energy boosts they have, but as the tykes grow older their energy level is apt to exceed their ability to expend it on their own. Adolescent Bichons will either unload those energy molecules under your supervision or they will devise activities of their own. Their chosen methods may not coincide with what you find appropriate!

Older dogs may settle into your lifestyle and be less "creative" in how they expend energy, but they may need encouragement to keep moving. Those of you who are over 40 might be able to relate to that!

So, young pup, middle-aged, or senior citizen, Bichons need exercise. Guess who'll need to be on hand to make sure that that need is met? You got it!

Have I discouraged you from owning a Bichon? Good! No one who isn't 100 percent sure should even *think* about ownership. The Bichon is not a breed for everybody and should never be purchased on a whim. That said, if you've thought this out very carefully and you're still with me, we can get on to the great joy, challenge, and companionship Bichon ownership entails.

Longtime Companion

The well-bred and properly cared for Bichon puppy will be with you for a long time. It is not unusual for Bichons to live well into their teens.

When my younger sister got married I gave her and her husband a Bichon puppy as a present. Their "Ami" lived to help the couple raise four sons and stayed on to join the family in celebrating a 17th wedding anniversary!

Obviously it is important that the puppy you select comes from a breeding program that has been carefully selected for longevity and is as free of genetic problems as possible. The puppy must have had the advantage of beginning life in a healthy environment and have been born of mentally and physically sound parents.

You will have to pay a respectable price for a well-bred Bichon puppy. Only you know what you can afford, but like anything else in life, you get only what you pay for. Believe me, there is no "bargain Bichon."

Know What You Want

The value of a purebred dog is its predictability. When purchasing a purebred dog you can be fairly certain of what the dog will look and act like at maturity. No purebred Chihuahua grows up to be the size of a Great Dane, nor is a Parson Russell Terrier ever the kind of dog to loll around the house with a lackluster attitude.

That said, within any given breed there are variations and different personality types. Let's take a look at the typical Bichon litter. You can be fairly certain, barring unforeseen accidents or unfortunate treatment, that each puppy in the litter will grow up with some similar characteristics:

They'll all have white curly hair.

All the puppies will probably grow to be between 10 to 12 inches (25 to 30 cm) measured top of the shoulder to the ground.

You can expect them all to have the same general shape.

They'll have dark eyes and noses.

They'll be amiable and nonaggressive.

What most people don't stop to consider, however, is that any of those characteristics can be graded on a scale of 1 to 10. Your Bichon puppy can grow up to be less than 10 inches (25 cm) or on the other hand a bit more than 12 inches (30 cm). Or any of their white coats might have minor cream shading in some areas.

There are also individual personalities within a litter of Bichons. It is important to talk about this to the breeder who has been observing the puppies as they were growing. If experienced, the breeder knows best how to match a puppy from the litter with the right owner. One puppy might need a drill sergeant personality for an owner, while the next puppy might do best with someone who is soft-voiced and gentle.

Mars or Venus?

Male or female? Although the sex of a dog in some breeds may be an

There are many endearing physical and mental characteristics that all well-bred Bichons share.

important consideration because of size or aggressiveness, this is not particularly the case with Bichons. The male Bichon makes just as loving, devoted, and trainable a companion as does the female.

I grew up believing the ideal housedog was a female, regardless of breed. Historically then, my housedogs were pretty much always females until I decided to cease breeding. The dog that I then decided to keep as a companion was a male. He turned out to be even easier to get along with than I could have imagined. With Bichons, I find most owners would take either sex before switching to another breed!

There are some sex-related differences to consider, however. The male has a natural instinct to lift his

leg and "mark" his territory. A male considers *everything* in and around the household a part of his territory, and he has an innate urge to establish the fact. This unfortunately may include your designer sofa or newly planted rose bush.

The effort involved in training the male not to do this varies with the individual dog. On the other hand, the girls have their own problems. Females have their semiannual heat cycles that commence anywhere from around nine months to a year of age.

During these heat cycles of approximately 21 days the female has to be confined to avoid soiling her surroundings with the bloody discharge that accompanies estrus. "Britches" sold at pet shops assist in keeping the female in heat from soiling the area in which she lives. She must also be carefully watched to prevent males from gaining access to her or she will become pregnant. *Do not expect the "marauding male" to be deterred by the britches!*

A good many of these sexually related problems can be eliminated or at least reduced by having your pet Bichon "altered." Spaying the female and neutering the male saves pet owners the headaches of sexually related problems without changing the basic character of their Bichon. If there is any change in the altered Bichon it is in making the dog an even more amiable companion. Above all, altering your pet precludes the possibility of its adding to the worldwide unwanted pet population.

Best Age for Selection

Raising a puppy is a wonderful experience. At times it can also be one of the most exasperating experiences you have ever attempted. In the end though, having endured each other through all the trials of puppyhood, you and your Bichon will forge a bond that has no equal.

Should you decide you do in fact wish to raise this bit of fluff from infancy to adulthood, be aware that most breeders do not and should not release their puppies until they have had their initial inoculations, which is at least 10 to 12 weeks of

Puppy vs. Adult

Your Bichon's age as it first enters your household determines how you will handle the arrival and what you'll have to deal with in the following weeks and months. You may decide a very young puppy will not work under your particular circumstances. A young adult, a mature dog, or even an old-timer might be your choice. (Don't discount the latter. Sometimes the older Bichon loses her loving owners and needs another good home to finish out those golden years.)

Like all living things, Bichons have different needs at different stages of their lives. They will react to their new environment accordingly and you should be prepared for this.

The male Bichon makes just as loving, devoted, and trainable a companion as does the female.

A young adult, a mature dog, or, in some cases, even a veteran might be a wise choice for those who do not have the time or patience required to properly raise a young puppy.

age. *Never remove a puppy from its home environment before it has been vaccinated!*

Prior to immunization, puppies are very susceptible to infectious diseases. Many such diseases may be transmitted via the clothing and hands of people. After the first series of vaccinations the breeder will inform you when your Bichon puppy is ready to leave its first home.

Show Dog or Companion?

If dog shows and breeding are in the future of your Bichon puppy, the older it is at time of selection the more likely you will know how good a dog you will have at maturity. The most any breeder can say about an eight-week-old Bichon puppy is that it has or does not have "show potential." If you are seriously interested in having a Bichon of the quality to show or to breed, wait with your selection until the puppy is at least five to six months old. By this time you can be far more certain of dentition, soundness, and attitude, as well as other important characteristics. No matter what you have in mind for your Bichon's future—dog shows or nothing more than loving companionship—all of the foregoing should be considered carefully.

If the excitement and pride of owning a winning show dog appeals to you, I cannot urge you enough to seek out a successful breeder who has a record of having produced winning dogs through the years. As stated, it is extremely difficult, if not impossible, to predict what an eight-week-old puppy will look like as an adult.

An experienced breeder, using the same bloodlines over an extended period of time, knows what clues to look for in selecting puppies with show "potential." Unfortunately, most prospective owners want both a very young puppy and some guarantee that the puppy will grow up to be a winning show dog. It is not possible to give that kind of guarantee, and no honest breeder will do so.

Price

The price of a Bichon puppy can vary considerably, but do understand that reputable breeders have invested

Responsible breeders do not release their puppies to new homes until the puppies have had their initial inoculations—somewhere between 10 to 12 weeks of age.

considerable time, skill, and work to make sure they have the best possible breeding stock. This costs a great deal of money. Good breeders have also invested substantially in veterinary supervision and testing to keep their stock as free from hereditary defects as possible.

A puppy purchased from an established and successful breeder may cost more initially, but the small additional investment brings you a great deal more for what you spend. A good breeder's knowledge of the breed and the bloodlines can save many trips to the veterinarian over the ensuing years. It is heartbreaking to become attached to a dog only to lose it an early age because of a health defect.

Expect to pay a thousand dollars or more for a three month old, pet quality Bichon Frise puppy. Older puppies will cost more. Youngsters with show and breeding potential may be double that price and young show stock five or six months of age will be still more expensive.

Where to Look

Caveat emptor is Latin for "let the buyer beware." Although the Bichon may not be as popular as some of the other breeds, it has already attained enough recognition to attract the commercially minded. There are those who care more about how much they'll make selling you a puppy than about what a good Bichon puppy is and needs.

Always beware of any "bargain basement" price you are offered to encourage the sale of a puppy. Successful breeders usually have long waiting lists for their puppies and have no need to resort to high-pressure techniques to complete a sale.

Even if there were no waiting list, no respected breeder that I have known would try to convince someone to buy a puppy who wasn't already sure about doing so. Don't allow someone to unload problems on you.

The only way a breeder can earn a reputation for producing quality dogs through the years is by maintaining a well-thought-out breeding program. Responsible breeders rigidly select the individual dogs for their breeding programs. Selective breeding aims to maintain the virtues of a breed and eliminate genetic weaknesses.

It takes a great deal of time, space, and testing to effectively conduct a breeding operation of this kind and it is extremely costly. Therefore, responsible Bichon breeders protect their investment by providing the utmost in prenatal care for their brood matrons and maximum care and nutrition for the resulting offspring.

Bichon breeders are particularly aware of how critical a well-thought-out socialization process is to the breed. Bringing together mentally stable parents is only the first step in producing puppies with good temperaments. Daily handling, exposure to children and adults, introduction to unusual sounds and sights as well as early grooming procedures are all important parts of the socialization process.

Only when responsible breeders feel the puppies have been given the benefit of the best care, nutrition, and sufficient human contact do they even begin to look for proper homes for each puppy in the litter. This may mean keeping one or even all the puppies in a litter until they are four, five, even six or seven months of age.

The only way breeders can continue to breed and raise Bichons in this responsible manner is to charge a realistic price for their puppies. A puppy with all these advantages costs more to raise and therefore costs the buyer more than a puppy from a litter that hasn't had this care and consideration.

The responsible breeder will not sell you a puppy whose sire and dam were never tested for any of the breed's genetic weaknesses. Nor will the mother of the puppy have been bred to a male of unknown mental stability.

Common sense tells us a puppy from a trustworthy breeder has a better chance of growing into what the breed should be than one who came about with only the dollar sign in mind. You should not even consider bringing a Bichon into your home that was not given these important advantages.

Unfortunately there are Bichon puppies that should never have seen the light of day. Hidden recessives in pedigrees can produce health and temperament problems that make dog ownership painfully expensive and trying.

The Recommended Breeder

The question is where to find a responsible Bichon breeder. There is no higher recommendation than that the breeder has the sanction of the breed Parent Club. In our case it would be the Bichon Frise Club of America (BFCA).

The recommended breeder is a member of the BFCA and has agreed to abide by the code of ethics established by that organization. The organization can provide you with a list of member breeders. Chances are some names on that list are located a reasonable distance from where you live.

One of the questions I'm frequently asked is how someone determines the difference between a "breeder" and a "backyard breeder." Can't a breeder keep his dogs in the backyard? If someone does keep his dogs in the backyard, does that mean the puppies aren't any good?

The purpose in designating some individuals as "backyard breeders" was to save dog buyers the anguish of bringing poorly bred dogs into their home. The term has little to do with the person's backyard.

I know of many highly respected and successful breeders who conduct their breeding programs from

Daily exposure and handling by both strangers and friends are important to a young Bichon's socialization process.

their homes, and their dogs do in fact spend part of their time in the breeder's backyard.

The Third Degree

Responsible breeders aren't invading your privacy with their questions about the prospective living conditions for their puppy. They are extremely discerning about where their puppies will live. Expect to answer a lot of questions about why you want a Bichon and how you intend to care for the puppy should they decide to let you have one. Get over the idea that you are doing a responsible breeder a favor by taking a puppy. If you do get that impression—scoot!

The following are topics most breeders will cover. Really you should be asking yourself these same important things.

An experienced breeder will normally tell you what kind of testing and what kind of guarantees they offer without your asking. Regardless, you should check these items against your own list to make sure that nothing has been missed or that you have not misunderstood anything. Details of the necessary documents that should accompany the puppy or dog you purchase are discussed in detail in Chapter 3, but what follows are items you should discuss with the breeder before money changes hands. This will insure a happy transition for your new Bichon regardless of age.

Health Concerns

Chapter 12 deals with a variety of hereditary health concerns that have affected the Bichon Frise breed at one time or another. This is not to say that any one of them affects all dogs of the breed or of the breeder you are dealing with. However, experienced Bichon breeders are familiar with these problems and are capable of discussing them intelligently. They will also be able to tell what steps they have taken to determine that their lines are not affected.

All responsible breeders will supply results of a veterinary examination revealing the current state of health of the dog you purchase. The report will also include a complete list of all inoculations that have been given, the dates on which they were administered, and when future inoculations are due.

Guarantees

Guarantees eliminate the possibility of misunderstandings and arguments over "he said, she said." If the guarantee specifies what the breeder is responsible for, there are no regrets or legal battles.

Most breeder guarantees outline the conditions under which the buyer may return the dog or puppy for a complete refund. If the breeder is willing to replace the dog or puppy purchased, the circumstances covering that possibility should be listed as well.

Pedigree and Registration Certificate

Purchase of a purebred dog entitles you to documentation of the dog's breeding. This is accomplished in the form of a registration certificate and four-generation pedigree.

Ongoing Service

Some breeders want to remain available for continuing advice or even care of some kind (i.e., grooming, training, etc.). If so, just what that entails should be outlined.

Qualified Input

Even if you've memorized every word of this book so far, there is something you don't know—something only the breeder can tell you.

The experienced breeder has not only observed each puppy in the litter from birth; he or she knows the personality of each puppy in the litter. Breeders know the bullies and the crybabies. They know which of the puppies will require a firm hand and which will need a soft voice.

When breeders have been given honest answers to all their questions they are able to determine which of the puppies in the litter would be the best choice for you. The bravest and boldest of the litter may have great appeal but might be too rambunctious for an elderly person or an invalid.

You might feel sorry for the little fellow who sits in the background while his littermates terrorize each other. However, the breeder may know he will never work out in your household of highly extroverted adolescents.

This applies even to grown dogs. People experienced in the breed know what traits to look for. Though your first impression may be entirely positive or entirely negative, a long-time breed authority may know things about the dog you would never think to question.

Flatter the breeder; pretend he or she knows a bit more than you do. Who knows, it could be true! If you do trust what the breeder feels would be the right puppy for you, it just might lead you to that storybook perfect friend and companion in a Bichon.

Show-Prospect Puppies

A show-prospect puppy must not only adhere to all the same health and soundness qualifications of a good pet puppy, it must also conform very closely to the rigid demands of the breed standard.

Chapter 5 goes into great detail regarding the standard of perfection for the Bichon Frise. The *words* of the breed standard are easily understood. However, the implications of the standard require a lifetime of study. This is why the experienced and successful breeder is so important to your quest when you are hoping to have a dog that will be competitive in the show ring.

Your chances of obtaining a Bichon puppy that will mature into a winning adult are far better if purchased from a breeder whose Bichon bloodline has produced many champions. But no one can be sure of having a winner until the puppy has reached maturity. Obviously a puppy six or seven months old or a young adult will provide much more certainty.

Humane Societies and Animal Shelters

Healthy, well-bred Bichons can end their lives in animal shelters for various reasons. This is why responsible breeders will insist they be given first opportunity to rehome any

A longtime breeder may know things about the puppy or dog you are interested in that you might never think to question.

dog they sell if the buyer is unable to keep the dog. Still, there are many Bichons to be found in city and county-maintained shelters. Should a dog in these circumstances be an option, it is extremely important to investigate the background of the dog and find out just why the dog wound up in the shelter.

This information may be available at the shelter or it may take a bit of private investigating. Regardless of how much time it might take, it is obviously time well spent. You are looking for a mentally and physically sound companion, not someone else's problem child.

Often local Bichon organizations can assist your search for information. Taking the time to investigate the dog's circumstances and history could easily result in your finding an outstanding dog that desperately needs a new home.

Bichon Rescue

Over the years, the Bichon Frise Club of America has taken an active role in responsible rescue of adoptable Bichons who are unwanted or abandoned by their owners. Through the effort of volunteers these unfortunate Bichons have found new loving homes. In January, 2003, BFCA established the Bichon Frise Charitable Trust to further assist in the ever-increasing need for rescue. The trust provides financial assistance to BFCA rescue volunteers and to non-member rescuers to efficiently house, rehabilitate, and responsibly place Bichons that have been relin-

A show-prospect puppy must not only adhere to all the same health and soundness qualifications of a good, pet quality puppy, but she must also show strong signs of conforming to the demands of the breed standard.

quished or abandoned and appear to have reasonably sound temperaments and health.

As the popularity of the Bichon increases so do the numbers of dogs needing rescue. Any single volunteer may have three or four such dogs in their care on a continuing basis across the country.

A rescued adult Bichon can be a perfect alternative for a family that does not have the time required to raise a puppy or do not want to go through puppy training. Adult Bichons adjust well to new environments and people and give many years of wonderful companionship. On average,

rescued Bichons are between three and eight years old, but seniors ten and over adjust nicely after a short period of time.

For information regarding the BFCA rescue program the organization's website contains rescue volunteer listings and provides a link to *www.Bichon.ResQ.org*. This provides online applications to adopt, listing information for placing a Bichon as well as a Volunteer Directory. Information and rescue referral can be obtained by contacting Gail Antetomaso, BFCA Rescue Coordinator by e-mail at *bfcarescue@optonline.net* or by phone at (516) 797-8790.

Chapter Three

Make It Official

Important transactions must take place before you tuck the puppy of your choice under your arm and head for home. Bottom line is that the seller will want to get paid. Cash is always appreciated, as is a cashier's check. The latter is recommended; it represents cash to the seller and provides you with a permanent record of the transaction.

If payment is a personal check the seller may wish you to pick up your puppy when the check has cleared the bank. Don't feel this is because you look untrustworthy. It is simply good business on the part of the seller. The breeder has little recourse if a check is returned and the puppy has left the premises.

Regardless of method of payment, request a receipt with an accurate description of what you have paid for:
• Date of transaction
• Amount received
• Breed of dog
• Sex
• Date of birth
• Registration number
• Form of payment (check number or cash)

You are entitled to four important documents the day you take your puppy or grown dog home: a health record containing an inoculation schedule, a copy of the dog's pedigree, the registration certificate, and a sales contract. These are supplied as part of your new puppy's identification packet. They will not only prove little Puff or Scamp is really yours but will also assist you in keeping the little tyke happy and healthy. The sales contract will help both parties avoid "I said, you said" arguments. There is no extra charge for these documents. Good breeders supply them with every puppy they sell.

Health Record

Most Bichon breeders have begun the necessary inoculation series for their puppies by the time they are seven to eight weeks of age. These inoculations protect the puppies against hepatitis, leptospirosis, distemper, and canine parvovirus. These are all deadly communicable diseases that will be dealt with at greater length in Chapter 12, "Genetic Diseases and Parasites." It is important to understand that these diseases can kill your puppy seemingly overnight, and even if the puppy escapes death it will invariably be permanently impaired.

A puppy should never be taken from its original home before these initial inoculations have been at least started. There is a prescribed series of inoculations to combat these infectious diseases, and it is extremely important that you obtain a record of the number and kind of inoculations your puppy has already been given. You must also have the dates the shots were administered and the type and make of serum used. Your veterinarian will then be able to continue with the appropriate inoculations.

The health record should also indicate what kind of veterinary treatment the puppy has been given since birth. This will include record of exams along with dates and type of medication used for each worming.

Pedigree

The pedigree is your dog's "family tree." The breeder or seller of every AKC registered dog should supply the buyer with a copy of this document. The pedigree lists your puppy's ancestors back to at least the third generation by giving each of the registered names.

A pedigree is read from left to right. The first two names in the first column on the left are the puppy's

Rabies

It is highly unlikely that your dog will be infected with rabies by another companion dog. However, this doesn't eliminate the ever-present possibility of your Bichon's coming in contact with wild animals that are always at risk of contracting rabies. Squirrels, skunks, and bats can all be carriers of this danger to your dog. Do not overlook the importance of inoculating against this possibility. A rabies inoculation is also necessary to obtain a dog license in your community, but in most cases the shot is not administered until a puppy is at least six months old. Local ordinances may have a bearing on this and the rabies shot may be necessary before that time. Check with your veterinarian, who will know the law in your area.

sire and dam. The sire's ancestors, reading left to right, appear on the top half of the pedigree. The dam's ancestors appear on the bottom half.

Most breeders supply the new owner with a typed or written pedigree. These unofficial documents give your puppy's ancestry, but like any document prepared by a human, spelling errors and other mistakes can unintentionally be made. If you wish to obtain an "Official Pedigree," only the country's official registration source can provide it. In the United States the two

CERTIFIED PEDIGREE

DIXIE BOY SCOOTER BLUE
NP02312901
BICHON FRISE MALE WH
Date Whelped: 06/09/2002
Breeder: JUNE C ARN

YOANNEWYN'S CAP'T BARNSTAPLE
CKC YL938548

CH CRAIGDALE YOANNEWYN EL TORO
NM50182601 (06-96) OFA29F CERF31 WH (CAN) AKC
DNA #V28194

KIBBATTS CRAIGDALE JOY
CKC WU853890

CH NUAGE CAPTAIN CHITO
NM76463801 (06-03) OFA58G CERF15 WH AKC
DNA #V32677

CH YOANNEWYN'S COL BILLERICAY
NM40332001 (03-96) WH (CAN)

CH NUAGE AMAZING ALEXIS
NM64521302 (04-98) OFA41G CERF78 WH

CH JOLINE'S THE WHITE MINX
NM24656005 (07-94) OFA32G CERF90 WH

DIXIE BOY SCOOTER BLUE

CH YOANNEWYN'S COL BILLERICAY
NM40332001 (03-96) WH (CAN)

CH NUAGE CHAMOUR DILETTANTE VAL
NM64521301 (01-97) OFA41G CERF78 WH AKC DNA
#V30317

CH JOLINE'S THE WHITE MINX
NM24656005 (07-94) OFA32G CERF90 WH

CH NUAGE DIXIE DIVA
NM79531101 (12-01) WH AKC DNA #V253781

CH CLARION CEZANNE DU CHAMOUR
NM33358703 (08-93) OFA24G CERF79 WH AKC DNA #V35414

CH NUAGE'S SUMMER SNOW
NM54200401 (03-97) OFA27G CERF71 WH

CH JOLINE'S THE WHITE MINX
NM24656005 (07-94) OFA32G CERF90 WH

Sire
Dam

The Seal of The American Kennel Club affixed hereto certifies that this pedigree was compiled from official Stud Book records on June 12, 2003.

The breeder or seller of every AKC registered dog should supply the buyer with a copy of the dog's pedigree. This may be typed or hand-written. A certified copy of the pedigree may be obtained from the AKC.

main sources for that document are the AKC or the United Kennel Club (UKC).

What a Pedigree Does and Doesn't Mean

All purebred dogs have a pedigree. It is the dog's family tree and proves that all the dog's ancestors are of the same breed. The pedigree does not imply that a dog is of show quality. It is simply a chronological list of ancestors—nothing more, nothing less.

If anything indicates one pedigree is better than another, it is the titles individual dogs in the pedigree have earned. Most of these titles are indicated on the pedigree, often in red ink. The titles and their appropriate abbreviations can be earned for excellence of conformation—"Champion" or the letters "Ch." before the dog's name. Other titles, such as those earned in Obedience, Herding, or the like usually follow the dog's name. Many of these possible titles are discussed in Chapter 10, "Together Wherever You Go."

Registration Certificate

The registration certificate is the canine world's "birth certificate." As with the Official Pedigree, the registration certificate is issued by a country's governing kennel club. When you transfer ownership of your Bichon from the breeder's name to your name, the transaction is entered

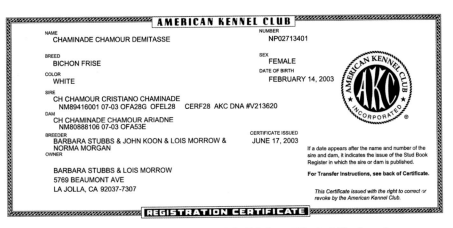

AMERICAN KENNEL CLUB

NAME
CHAMINADE CHAMOUR DEMITASSE

NUMBER
NP02713401

BREED
BICHON FRISE

SEX
FEMALE

COLOR
WHITE

DATE OF BIRTH
FEBRUARY 14, 2003

SIRE
CH CHAMOUR CRISTIANO CHAMINADE
NM89416001 07-03 OFA28G OFEL28   CERF28 AKC DNA #V213620

DAM
CH CHAMINADE CHAMOUR ARIADNE
NM80888106 07-03 OFA53E

BREEDER
BARBARA STUBBS & JOHN KOON & LOIS MORROW &
NORMA MORGAN

CERTIFICATE ISSUED
JUNE 17, 2003

OWNER
BARBARA STUBBS & LOIS MORROW
5769 BEAUMONT AVE
LA JOLLA, CA 92037-7307

If a date appears after the name and number of the
sire and dam, it indicates the issue of the Stud Book
Register in which the sire or dam is published.

For Transfer Instructions, see back of Certificate.

*This Certificate issued with the right to correct or
revoke by the American Kennel Club.*

REGISTRATION CERTIFICATE

The registration certificate is the canine world's "birth certificate." The breeder or former owner of a registered dog must complete, sign, and date this document and transfer it to the new owner.

on this certificate and mailed to the kennel club; it is permanently recorded in their computerized files. There are two kinds of registration certificates:

Litter Registrations

In the U.S. when the breeder submits an application to register a litter with the AKC, the information is checked, and if accepted, the AKC issues individual temporary registrations for each puppy in the litter. Breeders have two options when they receive these temporary registrations: They can use that temporary registration to transfer the puppy directly to you or they can individually register all the puppies in the litter in their own name first.

Individual Registration

Most breeders like to insert an official registered name for the puppy on the temporary registration, with their kennel name as a prefix. This then permanently associates that puppy with the breeder. Once a dog is individually registered the registered name can never be changed. You can call the puppy anything you choose, but its registered name is his or hers forever.

A "kennel name" is the prefix or suffix used to identify the breeder or kennel that bred or owned the pure-bred dog. This name is registered with the AKC or other registry, and no other dog may be registered with that name in the future. Most breeders add this to a dog's individual name so that it reads something like "Beau Monde The Brat" or "Romeo of Beau Monde."

When you purchase a puppy, the individual registration is transferred to you by the breeder. If you are given a temporary registration slip with your puppy, the slip must be completed and returned to the registry source

Are Vitamin Supplements Important?

Some breeders add vitamin supplements to their dogs' diets as a matter of course. Other breeders oppose supplements in light of the highly fortified major commercial dog foods. They believe oversupplementation can create skeletal and joint abnormalities. Be sure to clearly understand what your breeder's thoughts are on this issue and act accordingly.

with necessary fee no later than 12 months from the date of the puppy's birth. The puppy's birth date is printed on the temporary registration itself.

Sales Contract

Reputable Bichon Frise breeders supply a written agreement with the sales of all their dogs. The agreement or sales contract lists everything the breeder is responsible for in connection with the sale of the dog described.

The contract will also list all the things the buyer is responsible for before the sale is final. The contract should be dated and signed by both the seller and the buyer. Sales contracts vary, but all assurances and any exception to the final sale should be itemized. Some, but not necessarily all these conditions might be:

• Sale is contingent upon subject dog passing a veterinarian's exami-

nation within 24 to 48 hours after it leaves the seller's premises.

• Clear statement of refund policy.

• Any conditions regarding seller's requirement for neutering of dog sold.

• Indication that a "limited registration" accompanies dog (that is, the dog is ineligible to have offspring registered by the AKC or CKC).

• Arrangements that must be followed if the buyer is unable to keep the dog, regardless of length of time elapsed after sale.

• Provisions should dog develop genetic bone or eye diseases at maturity.

Sales contracts vary considerably, but the buyer should read the contract carefully to make sure it is entirely clear on what the buyer and seller are responsible for.

Diet Sheet

It stands to reason that the Bichon you've selected is happy and healthy because of the breeder's careful breeding program and the care of the offspring produced by that program. Your puppy has been properly fed and cared for every step of the way. All established and successful breeders have their own tested way of accomplishing this.

Because they have been successful in breeding and raising their puppies, most breeders equip new owners with specific care instructions. Each new owner gets a step-by-step record of the amount and

There are numerous details to consider and resolve before the puppy you have chosen is ready to go off to his new home. The breeder of your puppy can be an invaluable source for helping you to prepare for the new member of your family.

kind of food a puppy has been given and how this should change as the puppy matures.

Normally you will be given enough of the food the puppy has been eating to last until you are able to purchase the necessary products. Follow these recommendations to the letter for the first month or two. If there seems to be a reason for altering that plan I would discuss it with the breeder *before* making any changes.

A diet sheet should indicate the number of times a day your puppy has been accustomed to being fed and the kind and amount of any supplements that have been added to the food. Following the prescribed procedure will reduce the chance of upset stomach and loose stools.

Usually a breeder's diet sheet projects the increases and changes in food necessary as your puppy grows from week to week. If the sheet does not include this information, ask the breeder for suggestions regarding increases and the eventual change to adult food.

In the unlikely event you are not supplied with a diet sheet by the breeder and are unable to get one, talk to your veterinarian. He or she will be able to advise you in this respect. There are so many foods manufactured to meet the needs of all sizes, shapes, and ages of puppies and growing dogs it is impossible to list them all.

Like much else in life, you get what you pay for. There is ground meat and there is extra lean ground sirloin. Both come from cattle, but they are not the same. Chapter 6, "The Bichon Gourmet," takes a close look at proper feeding programs for the Bichon.

Chapter Four
Be Prepared

There are bridal showers, baby showers, and bridal registries. Why doesn't someone invent puppy showers? Then the new Bichon owner would save a small fortune and we could skip this chapter entirely. But if your friends and family haven't anticipated what the new little stranger entering your life will need, it's all up to you; and the operative word here is definitely *all*.

There's a lot to be thought about to be ready for the arrival of your new puppy. I seriously suggest you get down to making that list and checking it twice. Having everything in place before baby Bichon arrives will save you many costly days and sleepless nights.

You are going to need diversions to keep that little tyke busy, equipment to keep her in, and still other equipment to keep her out. There has to be a place for the pup to play and a place to sleep. You'll need some toys for training and some toys just for fun. The one thing you won't be able to find in any shop is patience, and that's what you'll need most. Patience you will have to supply yourself, and there will be times

when you will need more than you imagined possible. We'll get to patience later, when we talk about your kindergartner pup's first lessons. But first, the list, and then we'll go shopping.

The New Puppy Shopping List

If this is your first dog or puppy you will probably need to start from scratch and buy everything on this list. If you've had a dog before, check that what you have will adapt to the size and needs of your Bichon. A basketball might have been a fun toy for Bruno the St. Bernard, but it will probably be beyond what even a full-grown Bichon will want to cope with.

More expense? But of course, my friend—remember what I said previously about the costs of dog ownership.

Fences and Partitions

A partitioned-off living area will save you a thousand headaches. Paneled fence partitions, called

All puppies need diversions to keep their little minds occupied. They will need toys for training and other toys just for fun.

exercise pens, about three feet (92 cm) high, are available at most pet shops and are well worth the cost for confining your puppy to where you want it to be. The kitchen could be a perfect place to set up this area; your puppy will miss its mother and littermates very much and will almost immediately transfer this dependence to you and your family. Is there usually some member of the family in the kitchen throughout the day to keep the puppy company? Also kitchen flooring is usually easiest to clean up in the event of an accident.

This little fenced-off area tremendously assists pleasant introductions. Although children and Bichons are meant for each other, the introductions should take place slowly. Excited children are apt to grab for a puppy or chase the puppy when it runs. A terrified puppy can nip at a child's hands.

Bichon puppies are inclined to chase anything and anyone that runs. When children are frightened they run and scream. This incites the puppy's chase instinct even further and may create the urge to nip at the child's heels. The puppy is playing and the child is terrified. Supervised introductions are critical to avoid establishing a cause-and-effect scenario that might be difficult to change. With the puppy safe within its enclosure, introductions can take place slowly and avoid trauma.

This fenced-off area provides an area of safety for the puppy as well. Not only does it keep the puppy out of mischief but also protects it from being bothered (or bothering) any older or larger dogs in the house-

A partitioned-off living area will save the new puppy owner a thousand headaches.

hold. The adult dog with seniority may not be entirely pleased with the new addition at first. It is prudent to allow the two to get to know each other through the safety of a fence.

Puppies that have not been raised with small children may find these "miniature people" very frightening. Most puppies love children, but it may take a bit of time for the puppy not used to children to feel comfortable around them. The fencing keeps the children at a safe distance and gives the puppy an opportunity to accept them gradually.

Crates and Cages

Place a wire cage or the rigid fiberglass shipping crate inside the fenced-off area with the door open. This quickly becomes the dog's sleeping "den." These cages or kennels come in various sizes; while one which will accommodate the fully grown Bichon may seem terribly oversized for the very young puppy, you will be amazed at how quickly your puppy's size will increase in just a few weeks. This crate will also prove invaluable for both housebreaking and travel.

When I have recommended crates to some first-time dog owners you would think I had suggested locking their precious one in a trunk and throwing away the key. At first, they looked at the crate method of confinement (especially during housebreaking), as cruel. Once new owners have gritted their teeth and have done as I suggested, they invariably have come back to thank me. They agree the crate method is one of the most valuable training tips they have ever followed.

Using a properly sized crate reduces the average housebreaking time to a minimum and eliminates keeping the puppy under constant stress by correcting it for making mistakes in the home. Then too, there are days when everything and everyone in the household seem to be working at odds. The children need time out; you need time out. At those times there is no better place for the family dog than in its own little "den" with the door closed.

Most dogs continue to use their crates voluntarily as a place to sleep. Crates provide a sense of safety and security. It becomes their cave or den and in many cases a place to store their favorite toys or bones.

The fiberglass airline type crates are ideal for Bichons. A medium-sized crate (approximately 20 inches (51 cm) high by 24 inches (61 cm) wide by 30 inches (77 cm) long is the ideal size for the adult Bichon. Naturally this size is much too roomy for a very young puppy, especially one that you are trying to housebreak.

Bichon puppies do not like to relieve themselves where they sleep, so if the crate is large enough they will do their eliminating at the far end of the crate. A plywood partition can reduce the inside space as needed. If you don't want to start life all over as a carpenter, inexpensive smaller size crates, even used ones, can be purchased and discarded or sold at your next garage sale as they become obsolete.

Crates can be purchased from almost any pet shop and even in

Cages and kennels are the perfect answer for confining the new puppy when no one is around to supervise. They prove invaluable for both housebreaking and travel.

some major supermarkets. Do check to see if the manufacturer's warranty states the crate is "airline approved"—just in case you and your Bichon buddy decide to visit relatives who live across the country. When traveling by air such a crate is a requirement. Even when you decide to have your Bichon accompany you in the car, it is safest in its crate.

In warm climates, some Bichon owners prefer the metal wire type crates as they provide better air circulation. The wire crates come in all sizes as well and some have the additional advantage of being collapsible; they can be folded flat if you need to transport them.

Feeding Bowl and Water Dish

Select bowls that are nonbreakable. Many are constructed with wide bases so that they are not easily turned over. Many puppies find playing in their water dish great fun. The wide-based dishes are less likely to send water cascading over your

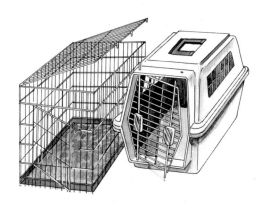

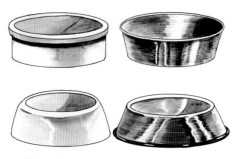

Select feeding bowls and water dishes with wide bases to avoid their being easily turned over by playful puppies.

floor—that is if your puppy hasn't learned how much fun it can be to dig in the water dish and watch the water fly out as fast as he digs.

Stainless steel or heavy plastic dishes are best. They are unbreakable and easily washed and sanitized.

Recommended Food

The breeder from whom you purchased your puppy has spent a lot of time figuring out what works best, so don't try and second guess that experience. Have a good supply of

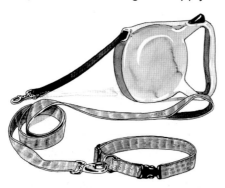

In order to accustom the new puppy to having a collar around her neck, purchase an inexpensive lightweight buckle collar made of soft leather or sturdy cloth.

that food on hand before the puppy arrives and you won't have to deal with puppy upsets and the diarrhea that usually accompanies those upsets.

The better pet emporiums carry an extensive line of dog foods. Check to make sure that your shop carries the food you need. Running out of the food that your puppy is accustomed to and substituting something different "just for a night" can prove to be more trouble than its worth.

Grooming Supplies

A Bichon puppy's coat doesn't require extensive grooming, but that puppy coat is gone before you know it and what grows in does require time. Chapter 7, "The Crowning Glory," discusses bathing and grooming in detail and includes recommendations for the grooming products to purchase.

Collar and Leash

The collar you buy that fits today will probably be in the garage sale bin in a month or two. Perhaps that's a bit of an exaggeration, but like shoes for kids, collars for young Bichons seem to be outgrown on the way home from the pet shop.

Just to get your puppy used to having a collar around her neck, purchase an inexpensive introductory lightweight buckle collar made of soft leather or sturdy cloth. The operative words here are *soft* and *light*. It will be the first collar around the puppy's neck and the less noticeable it is the better. The first leash should be flexible and very lightweight. (Actually you can survive those first few days with a piece of light cotton clothesline.)

When you first attach the leash to the puppy's collar expect the little tyke to act as if she is being pursued by a king cobra. Fear not, your little treasure will quickly get over seeing the leash as a death threat. Obviously, avoiding a big and heavy leash will assist the transition.

Toys

Bichons love toys and games. There is seldom any problem in enticing them to play, and once Bichons learn a game well, they become masters at coaxing you into playing it with them. Puppies have a strong need to chew and enjoy chewing. Chew toys help them through their teething periods and help them strengthen their jaws. Providing your puppy with interesting chew toys will save much wear and tear on your chair legs and first edition collection. But you have to choose the toys carefully.

Just because a toy is sold in the pet section of your supermarket or is marked "Towser Toy" does not mean that it is safe for your Bichon puppy. Never select anything that can be shattered or shredded if chewed.

Rope toys take a tremendous amount of punishment before they give up the ghost. They are washable and come in many shapes and sizes. The rope toys are shakable and very throwable, so outdoors is probably the best place for playing with them.

Bichons love toys and games. The proper toys also relieve their need to chew. Never select toys that can be shattered or shredded if chewed.

Don't think you are saving money by giving your puppy an old sock or discarded slipper. Everything you and your family wear or have worn will have those special smells and a dog is unable to tell the difference between a discarded old loafer and your new Prada pumps. Don't confuse the issue.

Painted things are also no-no's. The toy may be as colorful as Disneyland itself but make sure that color is nontoxic.

Teddy bears and other stuffed toys are not a good idea either. Your Bichon can treasure and care for a favorite teddy bear for months on end, then one day, teddy winds up inside your Ami's tummy. When that happens the three of you will all be at the veterinarian's office with your Bichon facing surgery.

Even before that happens your Bichon is going to feel duty bound to remove the eyes, nose, and squeaker from any stuffed toy

Post Emergency Numbers

Many households have the telephone numbers for their local fire department and police emergency contact posted next to their telephone. If you haven't done so, you should. Now add the emergency number for your local veterinarian to the list. Bichon puppies have a vacuum cleaner somewhere in their pedigrees and are constantly scooping up every imaginable item from the floor. If it's an object that fits into the mouth it's also an object meant to be swallowed—or so the puppies seem to think! Getting your puppy to the vet quickly may save her life.

immediately. That is part of being a dog and I think something they are taught before they leave their mother's side.

Chewing Deterrents

Your puppy will not spend her entire life inside the partitioned area. When on the loose, a puppy's curiosity and mischief level have no bounds. A puppy's safety and your sanity depend upon your ability to properly "puppy proof" your home. As you do so, remember what a Bichon puppy can't reach today, it will be able to bring crashing down tomorrow. Bichon puppies grow like little weeds and what you thought was out of harm's way might have been—a few inches back!

Electrical outlets, hanging lamp cords, mouth-size objects, and a host of other things you never considered dangerous can be lethal to an inquisitive and mischievous puppy. The trailing end of a tablecloth can risk bringing the entire table's contents down on a tugging puppy.

If you think of your Bichon puppy as one part private investigator and one part vacuum cleaner you'll have some idea of what to expect. With awareness you will be much better equipped to protect your puppy and your belongings.

You'll also need ties to keep those cupboard doors closed. Once a door is opened an inquisitive pup can find a treasure trove of gadgets and products to chew or ingest. Puppies can get into places that defy the imagination. Many cleaning products, gardening supplies, and medicines can be poisonous and must be kept in securely latched or tied cupboards out of a puppy's reach.

If kept clean and brushed Bichons have little or no body odor. However, the little "deposits" they leave behind do smell. Your supermarket has row upon row of cleaning and odor-reducing products that will take care of those little problems. Have such products at hand. I've found the minute I've said something like, "Oh yes, she's perfectly housebroken," a puppy is bound to prove we humans don't know as much as we think we do!

And the Most Important Items

The two most important staples you'll have to have on hand from the minute your new acquisition arrives cannot be purchased at any store. They are patience and persistence. The other intangibles, like experience, respect, and a resounding sense of humor come with time. Longtime dog owners realize the importance of the latter three, but they also realize without patience and persistence you can never achieve them. Experience has proven that good parents or people with good parenting potential often make good dog owners. They understand that owning and caring for a dog is not much different from raising a child. The difference is that children come to that place in life when parents can wipe their hands and hopefully say, "I've done a good job and now you are on your own." That day never comes with a dog.

Despite the fact that good Bichon owners make extravagant claims for their dogs they do realize that in the end, the owner is completely and totally responsible for the dog. A puppy doesn't learn until taught. A puppy, or grown dog for that matter, cannot eat until you feed her nor turn on the faucet when it's time for a drink of water. Dogs cannot let themselves out of the house to take care of bodily functions, and they don't have access to self-help remedies when they are ill.

You have to do all these things over and over—for the rest of the dog's life with you. And that is so whether you feel you are up to doing those things or not.

You're probably wondering if your Bichon shouldn't eventually get to a

Act in Bad Taste

A product called Bitter Apple (it tastes just like it sounds!) is available at most hardware stores and at some pharmacies. Bitter Apple is a furniture cream, but it is non-poisonous and can be used to coat just about anything your puppy might want to chew—electrical wires, furniture legs, what have you. In most cases the product will keep puppies, even grown dogs, from damaging household items. Do note that I said *in most cases*. I wouldn't be inclined to leave any puppy unobserved with some priceless work of art just because the object has been daubed with Bitter Apple. Some dogs, like some people, have very peculiar tastes.

If Bitter Apple does not deter, there is plastic tubing called "PC" available at hardware stores that can be placed around electrical cords and some furniture legs. The fencing panels we recommended would help keep your puppy out of dangerous situations and a daily "proofing patrol" will help you and your pet avoid damage and danger.

Odor Neutralizers and Cleaning Agents

Having a dog in the house does not mean the place has to smell like a stable. No one in your household would enjoy that and you can rest assured your guests will not, particularly those folks who do not like dogs.

You will learn that your Bichon is able to convey some of her needs to you. However, there are other times that it will be up to you to figure out just what she is trying to "tell" you.

what she does. Your pet may well use the same signal (a forlorn look, or a low-level whine or a bark) for many things—have to go out, water bowl is empty, and I need a cookie. Careful observation over time may help you discern subtle differences in those signals that will help you translate that secret language that dogs have.

Seniority and Senior Pets

Young puppies can be holy terrors and may take delight in chasing the family cat or harassing Rover the old timer who wants nothing more than to be left alone to snooze in the afternoon sun. When introductions begin this way friendly rapport may never occur.

Be smart—confine the newcomer and let the established residents take their time in learning to accept the new and sometimes not entirely welcomed new arrival. The pets in residence have given you their all, sometimes for years, and all of a sudden they have to share the household and your affection with an intruder. Be considerate and allow those with seniority to get used to the changes.

Keep the new puppy confined in its safe enclosure and the regulars will, through curiosity if nothing else, eventually make overtures of friendship. They won't do this, however, if you've allowed the new kid to pester them to distraction.

level of maturity where she can let you know what is needed. The answer is yes—sort of. You will have to make allowances for those times when you don't fully understand what it is that Ami or Puff is trying to tell you. There are those days when your Bichon will give you the "I need to go outside" signal and the minute you let her out she will turn around and demand to be let back in. Instead of accusing your Bichon of not telling the truth you'll simply have to mark it down as just another thing you're failing to understand.

Watch carefully and in some cases you'll be able to unravel the mystery of why your Bichon does

Chapter Five

There Are Bichons and There Are *Bichons*

Chapter 1 of this book followed the little dogs that were to become the Bichon Frise on their journey through the royal courts of Europe and by ship to the foreign ports of the world. We saw the hardy little breed spend time in Tenerife and the Canary Islands and followed them on their return to a Europe that was to be decimated by two horrific world wars.

Bichons survived by earning their keep as circus performers and by entertaining passersby as part of organ-grinder street acts. In the early 1930s admirers in France and Belgium stepped in to take the plucky little breed on yet another journey—the one to legitimacy. At this point began a developmental phase that led to the breed's becoming a popular show dog and household companion.

The fanciers of that time took the remnants of the breed off the streets, brushed the dogs up a bit, and sat down to put on paper what a quality member of the breed should look like. They were, in fact, writing a standard of excellence. In purebred dogs such descriptions are referred to as breed standards.

The Bichon developed some interest among European dog breeders but it was the Bichon's eventual emigration to North America that really began the breed's slow but steady climb back to the fame and regard it held back in days when it shared space on the thrones of royalty.

The American fanciers under the leadership of the BFCA realized that there was a huge disparity of "looks" in the breed and set about to develop some consistency. It is important to note the attempts were not to change the breed but to standardize and develop. There is a distinct difference between development and change. Development in a breed makes it increasingly more difficult to qualify as a superior specimen because more and more of the breed details have been fixed, and there is no excusing serious shortcomings in the perfected areas.

This illustration is used to clarify by comparison the many words used in the Bichon's breed standard to convey elegance. Note the smart and graceful look of the pony in the background and the lack of it in the more dwarf-like counterpart in the foreground.

The photographs of these two Bichons illustrate the point made by the two ponies in the accompanying illustration. Note the graceful elegance of the photograph on the top. See how it points up the lack of this quality in the photo on the bottom.

Understanding What the Breed Standard Says

The accompanying chart illustrates the various portions of the Bichon's anatomy that are dealt with in the Bichon Standard. A familiarity with these names will not only help clarify some of the points made by the Standard but also the names can be helpful in your conversations with the breeder from whom you purchased your Bichon and with your veterinarian.

If you're familiar with your Bichon's anatomy you'll be able to more clearly convey to your veterinarian or breeder any problems that your dog is having. Using precise terminology is far more likely to enable them to offer advice over the phone or in person if they know exactly where the problem lies.

Included here is an illustration of two ponies. It is used to clarify by comparison the many words of the

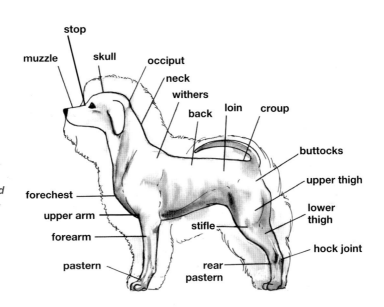

Learning the correct name for the various portions of the Bichon will help the new owner understand points made in the Bichon Standard. This also can prove helpful when having conversations with the dog's breeder and your veterinarian.

stop

muzzle   skull   occiput

neck

withers

back   loin   croup

buttocks

upper thigh

lower thigh

forechest

upper arm

stifle

hock joint

forearm

pastern   rear pastern

breed standard. If there is a single word that best defines the Bichon Frise it would be elegance. Note the elegance of the pony in the background and the lack of it in the more dwarflike animal pictured in the foreground. I have also included photographs of two Bichons that draw the same comparison.

What Is a Breed Standard?

A breed standard is a detailed description of an individual breed. It is meant to portray the *ideal specimen of that breed*. This includes ideal structure, temperament, gait, and type—all aspects of the dog. Because the standard describes an ideal specimen, it isn't based on any particular dog. It is a concept against which judges compare actual dogs at dog shows and breeders strive to produce in their breeding programs. At a dog show, the dog that wins is the one that comes closest, in the judge's opinion, to the standard for its breed. Breed standards are written by the breed parent clubs. These clubs are the national organizations formed to oversee the well-being of the breed. The standards are voted on and approved by the members of the parent clubs.

Official AKC Standard for the Bichon Frise
Approved October 11, 1988

General Appearance

The Bichon Frise is a small, sturdy, white powder puff of a dog whose merry temperament is evidenced by his plumed tail carried jauntily over the back and his dark-eyed inquisitive expression.

This is a breed that has no gross or incapacitating exaggerations and therefore there is no inherent reason for lack of balance or unsound movement.

Any deviation from the ideal described in the standard should be penalized to the extent of the deviation. Structural faults common to all breeds are as undesirable in the Bichon Frise as in any other breed, even though such faults may not be specifically mentioned in the standard.

Size, Proportion, Substance

Size—Dogs and bitches 9½ to 11½ inches are to be given primary preference. Only where the comparative superiority of a specimen outside this range clearly justifies it should greater latitude be taken. In no case, however, should this latitude ever extend over 12 inches or under 9 inches. The minimum limits do not apply to puppies. *Proportion*—The body from the forward-most point of the chest to the point of rump is ¼ longer than the height at the withers. The body from the withers to lowest point of chest represents ½ the distance from withers to ground. *Substance*—Compact and of medium bone throughout; neither coarse nor fine.

Head

Expression—Soft, dark-eyed, inquisitive, alert. *Eyes* are round, black or dark brown and are set in the skull to look directly forward. An overly large or bulging eye is a fault, as is an almond shaped, obliquely set eye. Halos, the black or very dark brown skin surrounding the eyes, are necessary, as they accentuate the eye and enhance expression. The eye rims themselves must be black. Broken pigment, or total absence of pigment on the eye rims produce a blank and staring expression, which is a definite fault. Eyes of any color other than black or dark brown are a very serious fault and must be severely penalized. *Ears* are drop and are covered with long flowing hair. When extended toward the nose, the leathers reach approximately halfway the length of the muzzle. They are set on slightly higher than eye level and rather forward on the skull, so that when the dog is alert they serve to frame the face. The *skull* is slightly rounded, allowing for a round and forward-looking eye. The *stop* is slightly accentuated. *Muzzle*—A properly balanced head is three parts muzzle to five parts skull, measured from the nose to the stop and from the stop to the occiput. A line drawn between the outside corners of the eyes and to the nose will create a near equilateral triangle. There is a slight degree of chiseling under the eyes, but not so much as to result in a weak or snipey foreface. The lower jaw is strong. The *nose* is prominent and always black. *Lips* are black, fine, never drooping. *Bite* is scissors. A bite which is undershot or overshot should be severely penalized. A crooked or out of line tooth is permissible; however, missing teeth are to be severely faulted.

Neck, Topline, and Body

The arched *neck* is long and carried proudly behind an erect head. It blends smoothly into the shoulders. The length of neck from occiput to withers is approximately ⅓ the distance from forechest to buttocks. The *topline* is level except for a slight, muscular arch over the loin. *Body*—The chest is well developed and wide enough to allow free and unrestricted movement of the front legs. The lowest point of the chest extends at least to the elbow. The rib cage is moderately sprung and extends back to a short and muscular loin. The

forechest is well pronounced and protrudes slightly forward of the point of shoulder. The underline has a moderate tuck-up. *Tail* is well plumed, set on level with the topline and curved gracefully over the back so that the hair of the tail rests on the back. When the tail is extended toward the head it reaches at least halfway to the withers. A low tail set, a tail carried perpendicularly to the back, or a tail which droops behind is to be severely penalized. A corkscrew tail is a very serious fault.

Forequarters

Shoulders—The shoulder blade, upper arm, and forearm are approximately equal in length. The shoulders are laid back to somewhat near a forty-five degree angle. The upper arm extends well back so the elbow is placed directly below the withers when viewed from the side. *Legs* are of medium bone; straight, with no bow or curve in the forearm or wrist. The elbows are held close to the body. The *pasterns* slope slightly from the vertical. The dewclaws may be removed. The *feet* are tight and round, resembling those of a cat and point directly forward, turning neither in nor out. *Pads* are black. Nails are kept short.

Hindquarters

The hindquarters are of medium bone, well angulated with muscular thighs and spaced moderately wide. The upper and lower thigh are nearly equal in length meeting at a well bent stifle joint. The leg from hock joint to foot pad is perpendicular to the ground. Dewclaws may be removed. Paws are tight and round with black pads.

Coat

The texture of the coat is of utmost importance. The undercoat is soft and dense, the outer coat of a coarser and curlier texture. The combination of the two gives a soft but substantial feel to the touch which is similar to plush or velvet and when patted springs back. When bathed and brushed, it stands off the body, creating an overall powder puff appearance. A wiry coat is not desirable. A limp, silky coat, a coat that lies down, or a lack of undercoat are very serious faults. *Trimming* — The coat is trimmed to reveal the natural outline of the body. It is rounded off from any direction and never cut so short as to create an overly trimmed or squared off appearance. The furnishings of the head, beard, mustache, ears, and tail are left longer. The longer head hair is trimmed to create an overall rounded impression. The topline is trimmed to appear level. The coat is long enough to maintain the powder puff look which is characteristic of the breed.

Color

Color is white, may have shadings of buff, cream, or apricot around the ears or on the body. Any color in excess of 10% of the entire coat of a mature specimen is a fault and should be penalized, but color of the accepted shadings should not be faulted in puppies.

Gait

Movement at a trot is free, precise and effortless. In profile the forelegs and hind legs extend equally with an easy reach and drive that maintain a steady topline. When moving, the head and neck remain somewhat erect and as speed increases there is a very slight convergence of legs toward the center line. Moving away, the hindquarters travel with moderate width between them and the foot pads can be seen. Coming and going, his movement is precise and true.

Temperament

Gentle mannered, sensitive, playful and affectionate. A cheerful attitude is the hallmark of the breed and one should settle for nothing less.

Chapter Six
The Bichon Gourmet

A balanced diet and fresh clean water are the key ingredients for proper canine health. Part of your Bichon's training should be to eat what you know is good for her, not what she thinks she might like to snack on from one minute to the next. Dogs are not different from children when it comes to food— dessert is more appealing than vegetables. Save treats for training sessions and don't offer them too frequently otherwise.

The Choice Is Yours

Whether moist or dry, there are basically three categories of generally available dog foods on the market: premium foods, "name" brands, and "budget" brands. As a rule of thumb, you get what you pay for when it comes to dog food.

Premium Foods

Often referred to as "prescription diets," premium foods are those available in specialty shops and from your veterinarian. They are considerably more expensive than the mass-produced foods you'll find in your supermarket. Premium foods tend to be more easily digested and in many cases are specifically geared to dogs with dietary problems. In the long run, the actual cost of a daily feeding of these foods is not much higher than other diets, because of the concentration of calories per cup. A cup of premium diet may contain 400 calories, compared to the 200 calories found in less expensive brands. Thus, you are feeding twice as much of the commercial diet to get the same number of calories.

"Name" Brand Foods

These are the commercial foods that you'll find in most pet emporiums and supermarkets. In most cases they are brands advertised on television and in newspapers and magazines. They offer adequate to good nutrition for your dog.

"Budget" Brands

Dogs can poorly digest low-cost or "budget" brands that even when fed in larger quantities fail to fulfill nutritional needs. Unless you are

Part of your Bichon's training should be to eat what you know is good for her, not what she thinks she might like to have.

able to carefully analyze the nutrients contained in these foods they may lead to problems. Fed on an ongoing basis some may lead to health problems that the average owner may not detect until serious complications arise. Veterinarians often diagnose gastrointestinal distress and skin problems in Bichons that are directly related to inadequate nutrition. It is pointless to feed an inadequate diet that must be supplemented with vitamins and minerals.

Who Has the Answers?

There is no infallible answer to the question of what food will best keep your Bichon in top condition. I have spoken to successful Bichon breeders throughout the country and each person I have spoken to seems to have an individual "best" way to feed. The best answer is, feed what works best—not necessarily what your Bichon likes best, but what is most apt to keep her looking and acting as a Bichon should.

Who can best tell you what food that is? I recommend you speak with the breeder from whom you purchased your Bichon. You decided upon that breeder because the adult dogs at that kennel were in good health and the puppies in the litter were equally healthy. The message in all that is whatever your breeder has been doing works for the dogs bred there.

The correct amount of food to maintain optimum condition varies as much from dog to dog as it does from human to human. It is impossible to state any specific *amount* of food your dog should be fed. Much depends upon how the amount of exercise your dog is getting uses up the calories consumed. A Bichon that spends the day playing with active children needs considerably more food than the house dog whose exercise is limited to a leisurely walk around the block once a day.

If there were a rule of thumb for feeding any normally active Bichon, it would be the amount of food the dog will eat readily within about fifteen minutes of being given the meal. What your Bichon does not eat in that time should be discarded. Leaving food out for extended periods can lead to erratic and finicky eating habits.

Use common sense. Your Bichon may have the constitution and appetite of a combat hero but burn only enough calories to accommodate an office clerk. Like any breed of dog (or their owners!) Bichons can gain weight very easily if their food intake is not controlled and they are not given an opportunity to get sufficient exercise.

Monitor your Bichon's condition. Don't be misled by all that hair—use your hands. You should be able to feel ribs and backbone through a slight layer of muscle and fat.

Dogs, whether Bichons or Great Danes, are carnivorous (meat-eating) animals, and while the vegetable content of your dog's diet should not be overlooked, a dog's physiology and anatomy are based upon eating animal protein. Protein and fat are absolutely essential in a dog's diet. The animal protein and fat your Bichon needs can be replaced by some vegetable proteins, but the amounts and the kind required in a vegetarian diet require a broad understanding of canine nutrition. The average dog owner seldom has that knowledge and even those that do are not inclined to spend the time needed to combine and/or cook the required ingredients.

There are available so many excellent premium and commercial dog foods that it seems a waste of time and effort to try to duplicate the nutritional content of these carefully thought-out products by cooking all

Tips for the Finicky Adult

If your new Bichon is an adult dog, retraining her food preferences may be necessary. An important fact to remember is that a healthy dog will not starve herself to death. The new addition may turn her nose up at the kibble you've chosen to give her, but trust me when I say she'll eat it when she gets hungry.

Offer small meals of the desired diet. Leave the food down for 20 minutes, and then pick up any leftovers. Do not offer any more food (including treats) until the next mealtime. A small amount of broth may be added to entice the finicky canine, but don't worry if your dog skips meals for a day or two. Healthy dogs can go a few days without eating, without long-term side effects.

A dull, listless dog that doesn't eat is another matter. For this, see your veterinarian.

of your Bichon's food from scratch. It is important though that you read packaging labels carefully or consult with your veterinarian, who will assist you in selecting the best moist or dry food for your Bichon.

A great deal of research is conducted by manufacturers of the leading brands of dog food to determine the exact ratio of vitamins and minerals necessary to maintain your dog's well-being. Dog food manufacturing has become so sophisticated it is now possible to buy food

Read Those Labels!

By law, all dog food must list all the ingredients in descending order by weight. As in food for human consumption, the major ingredient is listed first, the next most prominent follows, and so on down the line. A diet based on meat or poultry (appearing first in the ingredient list) is going to provide more canine nutrition per pound of food than one that lists a filler grain product as the leading ingredient. It also stands to reason that the diet based on meat or poultry will also cost you more than a food whose primary content is inexpensive fillers.

By law all dog food containers must list the ingredients in descending order by weight. This allows the buyer to determine just how much of what a dog needs for maximum nutrition is included in the product.

duce a tested, nutritionally balanced, high-quality food that is easily digested by a dog than it does to produce a brand that provides only marginal nourishment.

Look for a food, whether canned or dry, in which the main ingredient is derived from meat, poultry, or fish. Remember that you cannot purchase a top-quality dog food for the same price as one that lacks the nutritional value you are looking for. In many cases you will find your Bichon not only needs less of the better food, but also there will be less fecal matter to clean up as well.

Dog foods advertised and packaged to duplicate the look of a hot dog or cheese cracker are manufactured to appeal to *you,* not the dog. The better dog foods are not normally manufactured to resemble products that appeal to humans. Your Bichon could not care less what a food looks like. All the dog cares about is how food smells and tastes. So unless you plan to join your dog for dinner, don't waste your money.

Be careful of those canned or moist products that are advertised as having the look of "rich red beef," or the dry foods that are red in color. In most cases, the color is put there to appeal to you. The food looks that way through the use of red dye. Dyes and chemical preservatives are no better for your dog than they are for you and are bound to stain the hair around your Bichon's mouth.

Most respected dog food manufacturers now produce special diets for weaning puppies, growth, main-

for dogs living almost any lifestyle from puppyhood to old age. This applies to both canned and dry foods, but like most other things in life, "you get what you pay for." It costs the manufacturer more to pro-

tenance, overweight, underweight, and geriatric dogs. The calorie and nutritional content are adjusted for the particular level needed at each of these periods of a dog's life.

It is very important that you use the correctly formulated food for each of these stages. A food that is too rich can cause your dog as many problems as one not rich enough. Read the labels on the can or box, study the promotional literature published by the manufacturer of the dog food you are considering, and seek the advice of those who are experienced with Bichons.

Puppy Diets

Protein is an important part of a puppy's diet but it is not the only essential for growth. A good diet will consist of at least 20 percent protein, but puppies also need fat. Fat has the calories that a baby Bichon's energy-burning furnace needs to keep it stoked. Fat also produces healthy skin and helps build resistance to disease. Animal fats should make up approximately ten percent of the diet.

Carbohydrates also supply energy and provide the bulk, which is also a necessity in the Bichon puppy's diet. Potatoes, rice, even pasta are a good source of carbohydrate. Just be sure they are cooked well because a young puppy won't be able to process them if they are not well done.

Puppy foods must also be easily digestible and contain all the impor-

Avoid Food Stains!
There is nothing less attractive on a Bichon than having half its head stained red. A good way to test for red dyes in food is to place a small amount of the moistened canned or dry food on a white paper towel. Let the food sit there for a half-hour or so; then check if there is red staining on the towel. If the towel has taken on a red stain, you can be sure the color will soon appear on your Bichon.

tant vitamins and minerals along with calcium and phosphorus. Calcium and phosphorus are extremely important for bone growth. Both are important in that they work in tandem to do their job, but they must be present in the right proportions to be effective. Be careful here—too little calcium can subject a young dog to bone deformities such as rickets. Too much calcium is suspected of causing many of the bone diseases dog breeders are dealing with today.

Maintenance Diets

Adult Bichons do not have the same nutritional needs that they had as puppies. If your Bichon is given romps in the park, playing ball, and taking daily walks with you, those activities have to be supported nutritionally, but not to the degree that was necessary when she was doing all that and growing at the same time.

Maintenance diets are geared to provide such support. They are less fortified than puppy diets but not as restricted as what the aged dog requires.

The Senior Citizen

As Ami and Pierre age there is less activity and their metabolism slows down. Unfortunately, like their aging owners, the elderly Bichons will probably still feel entitled to the previous quantities of food. A "senior citizen" formula will enable you to feed your dog a substantial amount of food but will still cut down on calories.

Activity for the elderly Bichon may be reduced in intensity but should never be stopped. The old folks need exercise, albeit for shorter periods, but a nice long walk every day will do nothing but keep them healthier and you'll see how much they look forward to it. A word of caution here— pay attention to what it takes to tire the old guys out.

Special Foods for Special Times

The diets described up to now are those fed under normal conditions as your Bichon moves from puppyhood to adulthood and eventually to old age. There are times when diets must be adjusted to special situations.

When your Bichon is ailing, diet becomes a very important part of a cure. Sick dogs need a diet low in carbohydrates but high in vitamins, minerals, and fat. Rather than your attempting to mix food to accomplish this, you are much better off speaking to your veterinarian about a premium or prescription diet specially designed for this purpose. As a general rule it is best to speak to your veterinarian about foods if your Bichon is experiencing anything but optimum health.

When the "Baby Fat" Hangs On

Watch your Bichon's midsection. Bichons, young or old, don't become obese overnight. Excess weight comes on gradually and you may become accustomed to the gradual gains so that nothing seems out of the ordinary. Periodic hops onto the scale will avoid this happening.

Your veterinarian can advise you how much Ami needs to lose to recapture her girlish figure and how you can assist her to do so. Even though your own scales may lie when recording your own weight, the one at the veterinarian's office won't. Ami may seem fit as a fiddle, but I still strongly suggest biannual visits to the veterinarian for weight control and preventive maintenance. Practically all veterinary hospitals have scales especially for weighing animals and will have your Bichon hop on as part of normal hospital procedure.

If your Bichon is not overeating and is getting sufficient exercise, there may be some other cause for weight gain. Again, your veterinarian can look into this. As in everything else we've advised to keep your Bichon happy, healthy, and well behaved that "p word" (prevention) applies here as well.

There are available through your veterinarian prepared reducing diets that will keep the dieter satisfied but are low in calories. Their use will promote weight reduction without the chubby one's feeling you are running a concentration camp.

Exercise

Exercise is something your Bichon needs and it will also improve your health and state of mind. Fortunately you don't have to be fit for an Olympic marathon to give your Bichon the needed exercise. Good old-fashioned walking at a sensible pace is good for both you and the dog.

If improving your own health isn't incentive enough to get you out and moving, think about exercise this way—it's a nonprescription mood neutralizer for your dog. Bichons aren't like the herding breeds that need vigorous exercise, but they are energetic and that energy doesn't go away because you'd like it to. It will be used in some way, and if you would prefer it be spent chewing up your dancing shoes, so be it. Most Bichon owners would prefer to have their dog expend the energy load taking a good long walk or chasing a ball.

Don't expect your Bichon to get her necessary exercise on her own

Even though your scales may lie when recording your own weight, the one at the veterinarian's office is quite accurate. It will help to keep your Bichon's weight and general fitness under control.

unless there's another dog around. Even then the two probably won't be all that active once they get past puppyhood. As maturity and then old age set in, you'll find Bichons become less and less inclined to be self-starters in the exercise department. However, if you are involved, a Bichon of any age is ready, willing, and able to enjoy outdoor activities.

Puppy Exercise

Puppies at play with their litter-mates have frequent but short bouts of high level activity. This is nearly always followed by a good long nap.

Puppies play with their littermates at top speed, but this is always followed by a good nap. Keep this in mind when you or your children are playing with a very young puppy.

Puppies need exercise, but only as much as they themselves want to take, and then they should be given ample time to rest.

As soon as you and your puppy master the collar and leash technique the two of you can be off to explore the neighborhood and perhaps the nearby park. That is, of course, after all inoculations are up to date. This gives you both the exercise you need, and when you're out and about, you'll be working on your tyke's socialization process as well.

Don't expect a baby puppy to scale the nearest mountain with you. A smart puppy will plunk her little rear down and refuse to budge, and you will have to tote the little princess the rest of the way up and probably back down as well. Remember—brief periods of exercise with lots of rest periods.

Just as you should do for yourself, whenever you start a new form of exercise for your Bichon, do so gradually and increase the duration very slowly. I don't think it is a good idea to start jogging with a young Bichon—at least not before the dog is at least 18 months of age. By then the bones and muscles have formed and strengthened to the point where the jarring involved will not do permanent damage.

Regardless of age be sensitive to bone or joint injuries sustained in exercise or playing games. Always inspect sore or tender areas, and if they seem particularly painful for the dog, see your veterinarian at once. Concrete walkways and stony paths can be hard on the Bichon's feet. Inspect your dog's footpads often for cuts and abrasions if exercise takes place on cement.

Chapter Seven
The Crowning Glory

Brushing your Bichon daily will take just a few minutes of your time and will avoid your having to set aside a large block of time to catch up on those pesky snarls and mats that will always occur. This is a part of the necessary dedication Bichon ownership entails.

I do have one suggestion for the trimming part of your Bichon experience. Strongly consider having your Bichon professionally groomed for as much of the first year of his life as you can afford. I say this for two reasons. First, there will undoubtedly be a time in life with your Bichon when you yourself will be unable to get that necessary trim accomplished.

A trip to the grooming parlor will then be in order, and if your Bichon has never had this experience before this can be extremely traumatic. Not that your dog will be mistreated, but the strange equipment and strange people can be very upsetting to the inexperienced Bichon.

Secondly, being able to follow the trimming pattern set by a professional will allow you to do a whole lot better job than if you begin from scratch yourself. If you are inexperienced, your first attempts at haircutting might have little Pierre looking as if he's survived a hurricane.

Your Bichon will maintain the look that first attracted you to the breed only as long as you are steadfast in keeping the dog thoroughly brushed and clean. You must also either learn to do the trimming yourself or use a professional groomer.

Neglecting your Bichon's coat can result in the coat becoming so matted that the damage can be undone only by shaving it to the skin. This is not attractive nor is it good for your dog.

Your Bichon's coat insulates against both heat and cold. Shaving a Bichon "to keep him cool for the summer months" is working against the breed's natural defense against soaring temperatures. Don't misunderstand; you don't have to keep the coat long but there must be enough coat to protect your dog from the heat.

Care of the Puppy Coat

Most breeders have accustomed their puppies to being brushed on a

Grooming Equipment You Will Need

Consider that you will be using this equipment for many years, so buy the best of these items that you can afford. Quality grooming equipment not only lasts longer but also makes your job easier and more professional looking. Items you will be using in the actual grooming process are pictured on page 57, but there are other items you will undoubtedly find useful.

Grooming table: The first piece of equipment you should buy or build is a grooming table. A sturdy card table topped with a nonskid pad can be used, but the larger the area the more apt the dog is to try and wander. The important thing is that the table is at a height at which you can work comfortably. Adjustable-height grooming tables are available at most pet shops. Although you will buy this piece of equipment when your Bichon puppy arrives, the table should accommodate a fully-grown adult.

Nail clippers. The guillotine type nail clipper is recommended.

Thinning shears. These shears thin or reduce the volume of hair rather than cutting hair off in a straight edge. Useful under ears and in the areas where the legs join the body. These shears are also helpful in dealing with mats.

Straight scissors. Regular barber's shears are what you'll need.

Curved scissors. The curved blades are an excellent safety device for trimming around the eyes.

"Greyhound" comb. This is a medium/fine comb with teeth divided in half—one half are set very close and the other half set wider.

Electric hair clippers. This is an optional piece of equipment for the bottom of the Bichon's feet and around the male's penis. Scissors can accomplish the same purpose but the electric clippers (animal or human) do a much neater and quicker job.

Pin brush (also referred to as a "poodle brush"). This brush has long pliable metal bristles set in rubber. You will use this brush for your regular grooming sessions as well as brush drying the coat after bathing. Invest in a good one.

Slicker brush. You will use this oblong metal brush on your puppy almost exclusively and on the shorter hair and legs of the adult Bichon. It has curved pins set in rubber. This brush must be used carefully and gently as it can scratch the Bichon's sensitive skin and can pull out the adult dog's undercoat if not used with care.

Shampoo. There are many shampoos designed especially for white dogs—definitely the best to use for the Bichon.

Tweezers or Hemostat. Either can be used to remove hair that grows inside the Bichon's ears.

Baby or grooming powder. This is especially helpful to working out mats in the coat.

Basic grooming equipment you will need for your puppy grooming chores: nail clippers, thinning shears, straight scissors, hemostat, "Greyhound" comb, and slicker brush. A "pin brush" and curved trimming scissors will assist you in coping with the coat of a mature Bichon.

grooming table long before they leave for their new homes. Continue those grooming sessions or begin them at once if they haven't already been started. You and your Bichon will spend many hours at this activity, so the more accustomed you both are to the procedure the easier it will be for both of you.

Never attempt to groom your puppy on the floor. He will only attempt to get away from you when he finds something more interesting to do. You must teach your Bichon to lie on his side on the grooming table to be groomed. As the adult coat develops you will find the effort you invested in teaching your puppy to lie on his side will have been time well spent. It makes getting at those hard to reach places, like under the "arms" and around the genitals, a whole world easier.

Practice putting your puppy in this position a number of times before you begin the grooming process. Do so until your puppy understands what he is supposed to do when you place him on the grooming table.

Begin at the side front and make a part in the hair. Thoroughly brush that line out and then make another part down through to the rear of the

A hemostat or tweezers are handy tools for removing hair that grows inside the Bichon's ears.

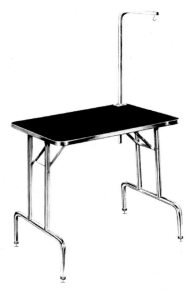

The first piece of equipment you should buy or build is a grooming table with a nonskid top. The important thing is that the table is at a height at which you can work comfortably.

of the hair. Do a small section at a time. *Part and brush*. Repeat this process, working toward the rear until you reach the puppy's tail.

Do the legs on the same side you have been working on. Use the same process, parting the hair at the top of the leg and working down. Do this all around the leg. Be especially careful to attend to the hard-to-reach areas under the upper legs where they join the body, as mats occur in these areas quickly.

Should you find a mat that doesn't brush out easily, use your fingers and the steel comb to separate the hairs as much as possible. Do not cut or pull out the matted hair. Apply baby powder or one of the especially prepared grooming powders directly to the mat and brush completely from the skin out.

With the puppy standing, do the chest and tail. When brushing the longer hair of the tail and face, do so

puppy. Brush through the hair to the right and left of the part. Start at the skin and brush out to the end

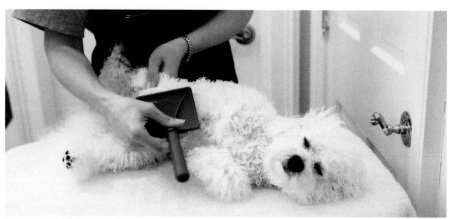

You must teach your Bichon to lie on his side on the grooming table to be groomed. Every bit of effort invested in teaching a puppy to lie on his side will have been well spent when the adult coat has come in.

This Bichon has been groomed in an easier to maintain "companion clip." This clip is too short for the show ring, but still maintains the correct look of the breed.

A Bichon will only maintain the look that defines the breed if he is regularly brushed and trimmed. This youngster has just been groomed, and is ready to walk into the show ring.

gently so as not to break the hair. When brushing on and around the rear legs, give special attention to the area of the anus and genitalia.

Grooming the Adult Bichon

What has been explained thus far may seem like a lot of unnecessary detail, but if you are both accustomed to the process by the time an adult coat has grown, you will thank your lucky stars for having spent the time. Not only is the Bichon's adult hair an entirely different texture, it is much longer and much thicker.

Undoubtedly by this time you have realized the pin brush with its longer bristles set in rubber is far more effective for line-brushing the adult Bichon than the slicker brush

that you used through puppyhood. The pin brush is also less apt to tear out the adult Bichon's longer hair.

The method of brushing the adult coat is the same as that used since your Bichon was a puppy. The obvious difference is that you have more dog and more hair. Ten well applied minutes a day with a brush plus a thorough weekly session will keep your Bichon entirely mat-free.

Nail Trimming

Accustom your Bichon to having nails trimmed and having feet inspected. Check between the toes for splinters and thorns. Pay particular attention to any swollen or tender areas. In many sections of the country there is a weed that releases a small barbed hook-like structure that carries its seed. This hook easily finds its way

Each nail of a dog's foot has a blood vessel running through the center called the "quick." It contains very sensitive nerve endings. Cutting into the quick causes severe pain to the dog and can result in a great deal of bleeding.

into a Bichon's foot or between its toes and quickly works its way deep into the dog's flesh. This will very quickly cause soreness and infection. Your veterinarian should remove these barbs before infection sets in.

Each nail has a blood vessel running through the center called the "quick." The quick grows close to the end of the nail and contains very sensitive nerve endings. If the nail is allowed to grow too long it will be impossible to cut it back to a proper length without cutting into the quick. This causes severe pain to the dog and can also result in a great deal of bleeding that can be very difficult to stop.

Should you nip the quick and bleeding occurs, there are a number of blood clotting products available at pet shops that will almost immediately stem the flow of blood. It is wise to have one of these products on hand in case there is a nail trimming accident or the dog tears a nail on its own.

Ear Care

Hair should be removed from the ear canal before bathing. Cleaning the ears is a vitally important part of Bichon grooming. If done periodically your dog's ears will stay clean and the process will take only a few minutes.

Begin by removing the long hairs that lead to the ear canal. If this area is neglected, accumulated hair blocks off the canal and serious ear problems can occur. Using tweezers or a hemostat or thumb and forefinger, pull out the excess hairs a few at a time with a quick pull. If using instruments, do not probe too deeply.

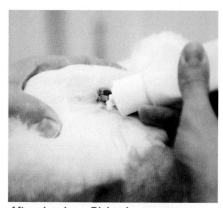

After cleaning a Bichon's ears, an application of bacterium-inhibiting powder made for the purpose will avoid ear problems developing.

After removing the hair, dampen a cotton swab with alcohol and carefully clean out the canal. Apply a bacterium-inhibiting powder made for the purpose and available in most pet supply stores. If heavy wax has accumulated or if there is an offensive odor, consult your veterinarian immediately.

Dental Hygiene

Regularly check your Bichon's teeth. Some dogs love to chew bones and hard biscuits and in so doing keep their teeth clean and healthy. That does not apply to all Bichons, however, and if yours is lax in the dental hygiene department, you will have to do the work.

Brush your Bichon's teeth at least once a week with toothpaste designed for dogs. Do not use toothpaste developed for human use as most contain sugar that will only add to your dog's problems. If plaque buildup has occurred, have it removed by your veterinarian.

Anal Glands

The anal glands are located on each side of the anus and must be regularly checked to avoid their becoming clogged. This can cause extreme irritation and abscesses if allowed to remain unchecked. Dogs seen pulling their rears along the ground are thought to be doing so because of worms. This is not the

Brush your Bichon's teeth at least once a week with toothpaste designed for dogs. Pastes and powders designed for human use contain sugars that will add to your dog's dental problems.

case and is more apt to be because of blocked anal glands.

Emptying the glands is an extremely unpleasant job because of the odor. You may have this done by your veterinarian, or if you wish to do it yourself, do so at bath time. With the dog in the tub, place your thumb and forefinger on either side of the anal passage and exert pressure. The glands will quickly empty.

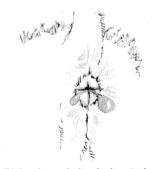

The Bichon's anal glands, located on each side of the anus, must be given regular attention to avoid their becoming clogged. The left gland in this drawing is normal but the gland at the right has become enlarged and needs to be emptied.

To avoid slipping place a rubber mat at the bottom of the tub in which you bathe your Bichon. A rubber spray hose is absolutely necessary to thoroughly wet and rinse the adult Bichon's coat.

In bathing, always start just behind the ears and work back.

Bathing

Never bathe your Bichon until his coat has been thoroughly brushed. A matted coat will only get worse when doused with water.

Place a rubber mat at the bottom of the tub to avoid having your Bichon slip and become frightened. A rubber spray hose is absolutely necessary to thoroughly wet the adult Bichon's coat. The hose is also necessary to remove all shampoo residues.

A small cotton ball placed inside each ear will avoid water running down into the dog's ear canal, and a drop or two of mineral oil or a dab of Vaseline placed in each eye will avoid having shampoo irritate your Bichon's eyes.

In bathing, start behind the ears and work back. Using a washcloth to soap and rinse around the head and face helps to keep shampoo out of the eyes, nose, and mouth. Once you have shampooed your Bichon you must rinse the coat thoroughly. When you feel quite certain all shampoo residue has been removed, rinse again. Shampoo residue in the coat is sure to dry the hair and can cause skin irritation.

Before removing your dog from the tub, squeeze out as much water as you can from the coat. It helps the drying process significantly

Use heavy towels to remove as much of the remaining water as possible. No doubt your Bichon will assist you by shaking.

Use heavy towels to remove as much of the remaining water as possible.

Using a Hair Dryer

Right after a quick towel drying, use your pin brush (gently!) to go through the damp coat to remove any tangles. Always set your hair dryer at "medium" setting, never "hot." The hot setting may be quicker, but it will also dry out the hair and could easily burn the skin of your Bichon.

It is very important to "brush dry" your Bichon using your pin brush (or slicker if the hair is short) and a hair dryer if you also plan on trimming the dog yourself. Allowing the Bichon's hair to dry on its own will allow the hair to curl, and it will be absolutely impossible to scissor the coat properly.

A dryer that has its own stand is well worth the money for Bichon owners. It will simplify the task by freeing both your hands to do the line brushing previously explained, and the more powerful dryer will reduce by half the time it takes to dry a Bichon.

With your Bichon lying on his side use the "line brushing" method you used before the bath. Point the dryer at the area to be brushed, using light strokes repeatedly until that section is completely dry; then move on to the next section. Brush gently and be careful not to pull hair out.

It is very important to "brush dry" your Bichon using a slicker brush (or pin brush if the coat is longer) and a hair dryer. You should begin your trimming immediately after drying to avoid having the coat begin to curl, which will make it impossible to scissor correctly.

As soon as your Bichon is dry, begin the trimming process immediately or the hair will start to curl and all your brush-drying efforts will have been wasted.

Scissoring

The main difference between the pet trim and the show trim shown through this book is primarily in the length of hair and the art of trimming. The finish work involved in the show trim is truly an art that takes years of training and practice. The pet trim is much shorter and easier to execute and maintain. If you plan to show your Bichon, engage a professional groomer who is an expert at trimming Bichons.

For home purposes, practice makes perfect. Look at the pictures of the well-groomed Bichon in this book and try to create the same

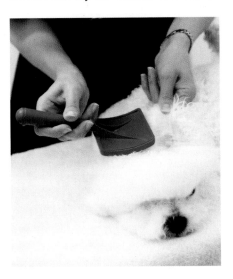

A. In order not to have the ear stand far away from the head, you must remove some of the hair along the neck under the ear. Facing your Bichon head on, your goal is to create a straight line from the outside of the ear on down to the foot. Begin the side trim under the ear and work down.

B. Continue scissoring on down the shoulder.

C. When you reach the foot, scissor around the leg to create a cylinder. Use the hair length on the outside of the leg as a guide for length around the entire leg. Once completed, go to the other side of the dog and complete the under-ear-to-foot scissoring and rounding of the leg.

D. If you have electric clippers, you can touch up that under-ear-to-foot line to make it straighter.

shape on your own dog. A tip to remember is to constantly lift the hair with your comb as you go along. This keeps all the hairs stand-ing directly away from the dog's body, and with practice you will achieve the smooth but plush look you are after.

The hair of the beard, ears, and tail is always kept much longer than the rest of the coat. The actual length depends upon what you find easiest to maintain. When you are trimming your Bichon's head the objective is to create a rounded look without any indentation where the ears join the

E. The next step is to trim the sides of your Bichon using the shoulder-length hair as a guide to length for the body. Continue right on to the root of the tail and down to the hip. Continue down the thigh and rear leg to the foot. Repeat that process on the other side of the dog. Round off the rear legs as you did the front legs.

F. Lift the front foot up and scissor to round the bottom outside edges to match the cylinder effect of the leg. Repeat on the other foot.

G. Repeat the rounding process on the rear feet.

H. With electric clippers or scissors trim out the hair that grows between the pads of the feet.

head. Though this sounds unimportant, it is one of the things that differentiates the Bichon's look from that of the Poodle.

To have the ear stand away from the head you must remove some of the hair along the neck under the ear. Face your Bichon head on. Your goal

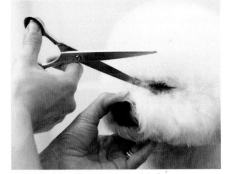

I. Head trim: Comb the hair of your Bichon's forehead forward toward the nose. Using the straight scissors, cut a straight line parallel to the forehead so that the eyes are revealed.

J. Step to the side of the head; and, using your curved shears, cut the head hair in a circular fashion from just above the eyes to the back of the skull.

K. Return to the front of the head, comb the hair up and out, and trim to smooth out the circular look as viewed from the front and from the sides.

L. Again, using your curved shears, trim away any hairs that stand out in front of the eyes and from the top of the muzzle.

is to create a straight line from the outside of the ear down to the foot. Begin the side trim under the ear and work down.

Continue scissoring down the shoulder.

When you reach the foot, scissor around the leg to create a cylinder. Use the hair length on the outside of the leg as a guide for length around the entire leg. Once completed, go to the other side of the dog and complete the under-ear-to-foot scissoring and rounding of the leg.

If you have electric clippers, you can touch up that under-ear-to-foot line to make it straighter.

Next step is to trim the sides of your Bichon using the shoulder length hair as a guide to length for the body. Continue to the root of the tail and down to the hip. Continue down the thigh and rear leg to the foot. Repeat that process on the other side of the dog. Round off the rear legs as you did the front legs.

Lift the front foot up and scissor to round the bottom outside edges to match the cylinder effect of the leg. Repeat on the other foot.

Repeat the rounding process on the rear feet.

With electric clippers or scissors trim out the hair that grows between the pads of feet.

Grooming the Bichon's puppy coat takes only a few minutes a day but those few minutes are important. They represent a training period for the time when the adult coat will require considerably more time and patience for both you and your dog.

Head trim: Comb the hair of your Bichon's forehead forward toward the nose. Using the straight scissors, cut a straight line parallel to the forehead so that the eyes are revealed.

Step to the side of the head and using your curved shears, cut the head hair in a circular fashion from just above the eyes to the back of the skull.

Return to the front of the head, comb the hair up and out, and trim to smooth out the circular look viewed from the front and from the sides.

Again using your curved shears, trim away any hairs that stand out in front of the eyes and from the top of the muzzle.

The photo above shows the completed trim. Look at your Bichon and see where more hair has to be taken off to give the finished look.

Chapter Eight

The Educated Bichon

You and I obey laws because we are aware that unpleasant consequences *could* result if we do not. We do not have to actually experience the consequences to know this is so. We know it because someone may have explained what the consequences could be or we may have read what might happen or perhaps even saw what might result in a movie or on television. We have the ability to conceptualize.

When it comes to our dogs' learning to obey "the laws" we know that dogs do it differently. We cannot approach them as we might in dealing with another person.

Some Things You Must Know

Words have no real meaning to a dog. It is what they associate the word *with* that counts in their minds. You could substitute the word "outdoors" with "chocolate" and as long as you use the word "chocolate" every time you take your dog out of doors, it would soon mean "out-

doors." Therefore, always use *exactly* the same word or words for what you want your dog to learn. Using different words to express the same command will only confuse. "Come" and "get over here" mean basically the same to you and me. If you've taught the "come" command, your puppy will have no idea what "get over here" means. Be consistent whenever you give a command.

Bichons are suckers for bribery. When Ami barks on command, she gets a doggie treat. She quickly learns barking equals treat. On the other hand, she learns she cannot bark her head off any time she wants to, because that will lead to a scolding rather than a treat or a pat on the head.

Avoidance will become one of the most important words in your vocabulary. Each time your Bichon repeats an undesirable act, the more difficult it will be to remove that behavior from her memory. Never allowing the unwanted act to occur in the first place will eliminate the need to "untrain" before you begin to establish the desired behavior.

Puppy Kindergarten

Socialization

If there is one lesson that all dogs must learn, it is to get along well with people. This does not mean a dog has to love every stranger that crosses her path. What it means is that humans lay down the rules and all dogs must learn to abide by those rules without hesitation. Your Bichon is no exception.

Temperament is both genetic and environmental. Poor treatment and lack of socialization can ruin inherited good temperament. A Bichon puppy that has inherited bad temperament is dangerous as a companion or as a showdog and should certainly never be bred. Therefore it is critical that you obtain a happy, well-adjusted puppy from a breeder who is known to produce good temperaments and has taken all the steps to provide the early necessary socialization.

Just because the puppies in a given litter are the result of such care does not mean socialization and temperament are finished products. Not by a long shot! The responsible Bichon breeder begins the socialization process as the puppies enter the world. Constant handling, exposure to strange sights and sounds, weighing and nail trimming are all experiences that help the growing Bichon understand that she was born into a human's world and that she is entirely safe when with human beings. The puppy is learning that after mom and her littermates, the best care and comfort comes from people.

At this early age everything puppies experience with people must be positive. Inoculations, a toenail nipped a bit too short—anything that causes discomfort for the puppy must be followed by reassurance and comforting to assure the youngster that all is well and the discomfort was not intended.

Puppies who have never seen a stranger until they are ready to go off to their new homes are a poor risk in the temperament department. Their ability to take in stride strangers and

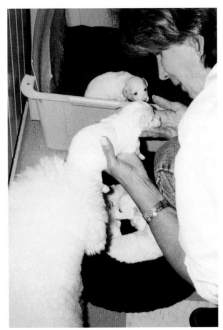

It is critical that you obtain a happy, well-adjusted puppy from a breeder who is known to produce good temperaments and who has taken all the steps to provide the early necessary socialization.

Good breeders always give their puppies an opportunity to explore new environments. If the litter has been kitchen raised, a trip outdoors, weather permitting, is arranged. This helps puppies on their way to meeting the world.

It is never too early for a puppy to learn the meaning of "No." Avoid punishment of any kind, of course, but gently guide your puppy away from danger with a firm "No!" to prepare her to understand she cannot follow every impulse.

Socialization of your Bichon puppy must continue when the puppy arrives at your home and, in fact, must continue through the rest of your puppy's life with you. It stands to reason you will not want the neighborhood waiting with the high school marching band when the puppy first arrives but increase new sights, sounds, and people each day.

What too many new owners fail to realize is that their new puppy, even adult dog, may well be happy as a clam living at home with you and your family. The picture changes drastically for the dog once she leaves the safety of her home if she hasn't had the benefit of the socialization begun by her breeder.

strange situations lacks cultivation. With reasonable care, after the puppies have had their first inoculations, they should be given the benefit of many new sights, sounds, and people.

Responsible breeders will also make it a point to introduce their puppies to new environments—if the litter has been raised in the kitchen, a trip outdoors, weather permitting, is arranged. One puppy at a time gets special attention in the family room.

At this early stage puppies are becoming accustomed to different tones of voice and voice inflections.

Take your puppy everywhere with you: the post office, along busy streets, to the shopping malls—wherever. Be prepared to create a stir wherever you go. Bichon puppies are real scene-stealers, and although some people might be afraid to approach dogs of other breeds, they never seem reluctant to stop and admire a Bichon puppy. Passersby will invariably want to pet your youngster. There is nothing better for the puppy than allowing the admirer to do so.

Carry treats with you when you go out. Should your puppy back off from a stranger, give the person one of the snacks to offer your puppy. *Insist* your young Bichon be amenable to the attention of any strangers you approve of, regardless of sex, age, or race. It is not up to your puppy to decide whom she will or will not tolerate. You are in charge. You must call the shots.

All Bichons must learn to get on with other dogs as well as with humans. If you are fortunate enough to have a "puppy preschool" or dog training class nearby, attend as regularly as possibe. A young Bichon that has been exposed regularly to other dogs from puppyhood will learn to adapt and accept other dogs and other breeds much more readily than one that seldom sees strange dogs.

Bichon puppies don't use great sense in whom they rush up to or what kind of dog they will challenge to a puppy duel. A puppy's unsophisticated overtures might be misread as aggression by an adult cat or dog and cause negative reactions on both their parts. It is your role to supervise.

What's in a Name?

Decide on a name for your puppy preferably *before* you bring the little one home because it is one of the first things the newcomer should become familiar with. Name recognition is the puppy's first step in identifying with her new home. Notice that after just a couple of days of hearing that familiar word, the young Bichon

will respond by wagging her little tail and giving you that, "Yes, me?" kind of a look. Use the name as often as you can. "Puff, come!" "Puff, outside?" Preface everything you say to your puppy with the puppy's name.

Historically the Bichon has been a fun loving, carefree kind of a dog. The dogs in your Bichon's ancestry were selected on the basis of their ability to entertain and enjoy doing it. They adapt easily to that role and that manner of learning. A heavy hand or Marine drill sergeant attitude on the part of an owner is contrary to the very nature of the Bichon.

Understand that different breeds react differently and need their own approach. I've owned Bull Terriers and those of us who know the breed are aware that figuratively it takes

There is nothing better for your puppy than meeting strangers of all ages. She should become accustomed to the touch of friends outside of your family circle.

Decide on a name for your new puppy as soon as possible. Name recognition is the puppy's first step in identifying with her new home.

a brick wall falling down on a "Bully" to get its attention. For a German Shepherd or Doberman Pinscher a demanding owner is their cup of tea—they thrive on it. But you don't have a Bull Terrier, German Shepherd, or Doberman—you have a Bichon Frise.

Think Ahead

A new puppy is capable of finding its way into situations you never thought any dog could contrive, much less one so young. You've probably also begun to think keeping ahead of all this is not much easier than training for the next Olympiad.

Bringing a new dog of any age into your home presents transition problems that have to be dealt with. We've emphasized the value of preparation and patience, so think ahead, read, and ask advice from the breeder of your puppy. Breeders have lived through the growth transitions of scores of dogs, and if anyone can give you workable suggestions it is the person who has gone through it all.

Not only does the breeder from whom you are getting your Bichon understand how the breed in general reacts to most situations, but also the specific puppy you are taking home. Believe me, having input on those two things can save you many headaches.

Keep in mind that to the new Bichon puppy everything in your home is entirely strange. On top of that there are no littermates or familiar sights or smells to tell the youngster, "You are not alone, and all is well." Beginning with the first day your new Bichon enters your home, keep in mind two very important facts:

• Do not let your puppy do *anything* on the first day or days that you will not want her to do for the rest of the time the two of you are living together.

• Never be severe in correcting unwanted behavior.

Try to avoid nagging and correcting the newcomer every time the puppy turns around. New dogs, regardless of age, will make mistakes, but do realize they do not know the rules yet. You're probably wondering though, how you can avoid bad habits establishing themselves without constantly correcting your Bichon. The answer is actually quite simple. Avoid putting the new dog into situations where she will be breaking the rules.

A puppy that is asleep in her crate when you can't be there to supervise or in a nearby enclosure where you can still be seen when you don't need her underfoot isn't being cruelly treated. Such an arrangement can eliminate the necessity of your being a nag and at the same time will avoid confusing your puppy by making it okay to do one thing today and wrong to do it tomorrow.

The First Few Days and Weeks

Night Cries

The safest way to transport the puppy from kennel to your home is to obtain a pet carrier or cardboard box large enough for the puppy to stretch out comfortably with sides high enough so that she cannot climb out. Put a layer of newspapers at the bottom in case of accidents and a soft blanket or towel on top of that. Ideally another family member or friend should accompany you to do the driving or hold the carrier that the puppy is in.

All the better if you can hold the box on your lap. That way it will be your reassuring hand that will be the first to stroke the puppy as she becomes accustomed to the strange and ever-changing new world.

The first few days and weeks are tough, especially for a very young puppy. When you take a puppy away from her littermates and put her into an entirely strange environment, the baby is going to be confused and lonely. No warm bodies to snuggle up to—no playmates for games. During the day is bad enough, but nights seem even worse. Your thinking ahead can alleviate some of the transition trauma for your puppy.

For the first few nights after the new puppy arrives put her sleeping box next to your bed. If the newcomer wakes up crying in loneliness, a reassuring hand can be dropped down into the box and you've

When a puppy is taken away from her littermates, she will be confused and lonely. During the day is bad enough, but nights seem even worse. Thinking ahead can alleviate some of the transition trauma she will experience.

avoided having to trudge to the kitchen to quiet the lonely puppy.

Is this establishing a bad precedent? Actually not—the puppy has no idea *where* she is when she's in the box. She knows a reassuring hand drops down, but that is from the great beyond as far as she is concerned. After a night or two you'll find your light tap on the box will make whimpers quickly subside. Soon the puppy learns to sleep through the night in the comfort and safety of her little "den."

Once the pup has learned its perfectly safe to be alone, the box can be shifted to the kitchen enclosure and the shipping kennel eventually substituted for the box. Ideally, you

should try to collect your puppy from the breeder in the morning to allow at least one full day to adjust to the overwhelming new world. It won't be *quite* as bad when night falls.

Vacation Time

Do your best to have your Bichon puppy come to live with you when you or another family member has a week or at least a few days off. Summer vacation time is good; holidays not so good—it's too hectic. Being with the pup most of the time those first few days helps tremendously. By the time a week has gone by, your puppy will have begun to forget all about littermates and will begin to become a member of your family, even if the "family" is just the two of you.

If you can't manage a week off, try taking a Friday off and picking the puppy up early that day. It will give the two of you a full three days to get past that difficult transition.

The breeder may have started a housebreaking routine with your puppy. If so, check to learn just how this was being done so that you can be consistent. If your puppy has been accustomed to relieving herself outdoors, don't expect her to understand you want her to use newspapers indoors. If the situation is reversed and you want her to eliminate only outdoors, take newspapers with you at first and put them down where you want the puppy to take care of her duties. You can eliminate the papers later.

Everything is new for the puppy and every household rule has to be learned. Make everyone in your home understand that it is critical to keep the rules the same. A puppy won't understand that it is all right to lounge on the sofa with the kids but not all right when mom is home.

Persistence

Never let your Bichon get the idea that if it is persistent enough it will triumph. Once the puppy gets this idea locked in her little head, life becomes a nightmare, because the little monster will apply what she has learned to everything she wants or doesn't want. Nip this behavior in the bud; the sooner you start, the

Danger Lurks Outdoors

People who live in areas where coyotes are present must *never* leave their Bichon outdoors alone! This particularly applies to puppies, but coyotes have been known to run off with fully mature dogs the size of Bichons. Owners of small dogs who put their dogs out and turned their backs "just for a minute" have reported far too many coyote snatches. If predators of this kind are known to live in your area, exercise your Bichon outdoors *on a leash* with the leash in hand.

easier the demanding behavior will be to correct.

Begin by confining your pup to its crate while you are in the same room. Some puppies will be fine as long as they can see you. Others may decide they can be happy only under your feet. If the puppy begins to whine or bark, give a sharp *"Quiet!"* command. Usually that does the trick. If not, it may require rapping the crate with the flat of your hand when you give the command. Almost invariably the noise and simultaneous command will make the puppy pause, if not stop entirely.

You must have the last word, and if you are persistent you will definitely win. Do not pick the puppy up to comfort her. This is exactly what the complainer is after and you will be teaching the puppy that the way to get what she wants is to be vocal about it.

Do Bichons Housebreak Easily?

In a word—*no*. Some Bichons, but fortunately not all of them, call upon all your patience reserves. Males have proven easier to housebreak than their sisters. You just never know how quickly your puppy will get the message until she *gets the message*. But if *you* aren't persistent, the two of you may deal with housebreaking for what will seem like an eternity.

Sometimes, with the more tenacious little fellows, sterner measures are necessary. Purchase a plastic spray bottle or water gun and fill it with water, adjusting the spray to a steady stream. The minute the barking or whining begins, command "Quiet!" and give the puppy a shot directly in her face. No harm is done, but puppies (even grown dogs) hate this. A few rounds with the water treatment usually get the message across.

Basic Training

Housebreaking

Avoiding the problem is the easiest way to approach this particular phase of your puppy's training. When it's time to go, a puppy will be inclined to return to the same area she has relieved herself previously. If that's in the middle of your new cream-colored Oriental rug, so be it. The puppy won't mind. But if the proper spot with all the right smells is outdoors, the puppy will begin to develop a vague yearning for that spot. A mild—and in the case of some Bichons, *very mild*—distressed expression and perhaps a little whine will occur seconds before "it" happens. As puppies begin to associate "going" with that spot outdoors or on the newspapers, they usually become more and more insistent that they be given access to that spot.

The Avoidance Method

The method of housebreaking I recommend is avoidance, and it involves use of the shipping kennel or crate you purchased on your initial shopping spree. Begin using the crate to feed your Bichon puppy. Keep the door closed and latched while the puppy is eating. When the meal is finished, open the cage and *carry* the puppy outdoors to the spot where you want the puppy to learn to eliminate.

In the event you do not have outdoor access or if you will be away from home for long periods of time, begin housebreaking by placing newspapers in some out of the way corner that is easily accessible for the puppy. If you consistently take your puppy to the same spot you will reinforce the habit of going there for that purpose.

It is important that you do not let the puppy loose after eating. Young puppies will eliminate almost immediately after eating or drinking. They will also be ready to relieve themselves when they first wake up and after playing. If you keep a watchful eye on your puppy you will quickly learn when this is about to take place. *Do not give your puppy an opportunity to learn that she can eliminate in the house!* Your house training chores will be reduced considerably if you avoid the beginning of bad habits.

If you are not able to watch your puppy every minute, the puppy should be in her cage or crate with the door securely latched. Each time you put your puppy in the crate give her a small treat. Throw the treat to the back of the cage and encourage the puppy to walk in on her own. When she does so, praise her to the sky and perhaps even offer another treat through the wires of the cage.

Do understand a Bichon puppy of eight to twelve weeks will not be able to contain itself for long periods of time. Puppies of that age must relieve themselves often except at night. Your schedule must be adjusted accordingly. Also make sure your puppy has relieved herself at night before the last member of the family retires.

Your first priority in the morning is to get the puppy outdoors. Just how early this will be depends much more upon your puppy than upon you. If your Bichon is like most others there will be no doubt in your mind when it needs to be let out. You will also very quickly learn to tell the difference between the puppy's "emergency" signals and just unhappy grumbling. Do not test your puppy's ability to hang in there. A puppy's vocal demand to be let out is confirmation that the housebreaking lesson is being learned.

Should you find it necessary to be away from home all day, you will not be able to leave your puppy in a crate. But on the other hand, do not make the mistake of allowing it to roam the house or even large rooms at will—*you will never get a housebreaking routine established!*

Confine the puppy to a small room or partitioned area and cover the floor with newspaper. Make this area large enough so that the puppy will not have to relieve herself next to her bed, food, or water bowls. In most cases you will find the puppy will be inclined to use one particular spot to perform her bowel and bladder functions.

When it's time to relieve herself, a puppy will be inclined to return to the area she has used previously. If the proper spot with all the right smells is outdoors or papers in the laundry room, the puppy will develop a vague yearning for that spot. It is up to you to detect that yearning!

Words of Caution on Dogs and Cars

Riding loose. As much as it might seem more enjoyable to have your puppy or adult dog ride loose in the car or on the seat beside you, this can be extremely dangerous. An overly enthusiastic canine passenger can interfere with the driver's control or divert the driver's attention. Also, a sudden stop can hurl your dog against the front window, severely injuring or even killing him.

The safest way to transport your dog is in a carrier with the door securely latched. Many station wagons accommodate partitions commonly referred to as dog guards. These safety devices confine dogs to the rear portion of the car. These simple safety precautions might one day save the life of your pet.

I.D. Tags. Any time your dog leaves your home, she should be wearing a collar with identification tags and license attached. Many times dogs are thrown clear of the car in an accident but become so frightened that they run blindly away. Not knowing where they are and not carrying any means of identification means a dog may be lost forever.

Temperature control. It is important to make it a practice to never leave your dog alone in the car with the windows closed. Even on cooler days, the sun beating down on a closed car can send the inside temperature soaring. Leaving a dog alone in an unventilated car could easily cause her death.

The only time a dog may be left alone in a car is when temperature conditions permit the windows to be left open. But this in itself is dangerous, because open windows risk your dog's escape and invite theft. Thieves are not beyond stealing dogs—especially friendly Bichons! A loose dog in a car with open windows courts disaster.

When you are home and the puppy is not enclosed in her regular space, you must take her to this exact spot to eliminate at the appropriate time. Although it is much easier to reliably housebreak a puppy when someone is usually home, it is not impossible for the person or family that is away all day to also do so. It just takes more time and patience and an eagle eye when the puppy is not in her enclosure.

Car Travel

Trips to the shopping mall or walks through the park will expose your young dog to new and different situations each time you are out. Of course, this should never be attempted until your puppy has had all of her inoculations. Once that is completed, you are both ready to set off to meet the world, and this often involves riding in a car.

It's best not to plan a coast-to-coast trip with a puppy that hasn't become accustomed to riding in a car. Some dogs are subject to motion sickness, and the only way to get by that problem is to begin with short jaunts of a few minutes and gradually lengthen the time. Puppies that are first-time riders or those that are subject to becoming carsick should not be fed or watered for a minimum of at least three to four hours before they take that trip. A full stomach can worsen an already difficult situation for these delicate canines.

When the puppy seems to accept short rides happily, the length of time in the car can be increased gradually until you see that the puppy is truly enjoying the outings. Even those dogs and puppies suffering from the most severe cases of carsickness seem to respond to this approach and soon begin to consider the car a second home. If your dog's carsickness continues, speak to your veterinarian, who can prescribe medication to alleviate the problem.

Chewing

Your new puppy won't be in her new home very long before you'll realize that puppies love to chew. Grown dogs will chew. The senior citizens will chew (if they have any teeth). The difference is that you will have taught your adult Bichon what it may and may not chew. The puppy hasn't learned this yet, and it is one lesson that could be costly if not learned.

Some breeds have a stronger chewing need than others do. When your Bichon puppy chews you might miss the evidence her little teeth make. If the habit is left unchecked, however, you may live to find the leg of your priceless antique table chewed nearly through. Never underestimate the power of those little jaws!

Don't leave your new pigskin gloves on the floor or within reach of your puppy and then have a coronary because your puppy has used them as a chew stick. Be kind enough to your puppy to avoid leaving temptation in her path, especially during teething time.

A word to the wise—bored Bichons are capable of renovating an entire household in a relatively short time. You have two choices: either empty your entire household of anything you value or put your Bichon in her crate where she won't be tempted to demolish your antique collection while you are out shopping.

Yes, Bitter Apple and things like tobacco sauce and other deterrents can help, but you can't drench your entire household with these products. Confinement with an enjoyable chew toy when you can't keep an eye on your puppy is the wisest approach. Even when you are at home, always have something safe available for the puppy to chew on.

Separation Anxiety

Separation anxiety is a far greater problem than what most dog owners realize. This anxiety can be exhibited in endless barking or extremely destructive or neurotic behavior when the owner is absent. All too often this is dismissed as a temper tantrum done out of spite or because the dog is just plain destructive. Animal shelter groups say this problem is one that is most apt to have owners abandon their dogs or leave them to rescue organizations.

In most cases behavior of this kind is due to the dog's uncontrollable fear of being left alone. The behavior is almost to be expected from dogs that have been abandoned at some point

Separation anxiety is a far greater problem than most dog owners realize. It can manifest itself in many ways, from incessant barking to destructive behavior. For extreme cases of separation anxiety, there is a relatively new drug called Comicalm that helps to relieve the problem.

in their lives. Some dogs that have been forced to undergo an extreme change in their living conditions will also exhibit this neurotic and destructive behavior.

Without realizing it owners themselves can create or compound the problem by their own behavior. The last thing you want to do is contribute to your dog's insecurity by making your departure or return comparable to a soap opera cliff-hanger. Don't make leaving a major event—just go.

Nor should you make your return a spectacle. In fact, with a dog that is manifesting separation anxiety symptoms, it is wise to completely ignore the dog for 10 or 15 minutes after you do get back.

There is a relatively new drug called Comicalm that helps to relieve the separation anxiety problem so that gradual retraining can take place. The drug is actually an antidepressant or mood leveler that works in much the same way as its human counterpart Prozac. Should your Bichon be experiencing stress of this kind and your efforts without medication have proven futile, speak to your veterinarian about the possibility of using Comicalm.

Here again we have another vote for the intelligent use of your Bichon's shipping crate or kennel. It makes sense to confine all dogs to a safe area while you are away, but it is especially important to do so with a dog undergoing separation anxiety. Rather than giving the dog yet another opportunity to reinforce her neurotic behavior—*avoid!*

Chapter Nine

School Days

A Bichon puppy's attention span is very short. Don't forget, a very young puppy is not going to understand the more complex commands an older dog will eventually learn to respond to. This does not mean you should delay simple basic training. As soon as you bring your puppy home, household rules begin. It will be much harder on the puppy to be reprimanded today for something it was perfectly okay to do yesterday.

It's All in the Approach

Humans have the option of changing their minds. What seems the thing to do today may have no appeal tomorrow. Unfortunately your Bichon can't relate to that entirely human concept. For dogs it's all a matter of black and white—you may or you may not, yes or no. Your understanding (and believing!) that will take you a long way in getting your message across to your Bichon student.

If you use the proper approach, any dog that is not mentally deficient can be taught to be a good canine citizen. Many dog owners do not understand how a dog learns, nor do they realize they can and should be breed specific in their approach to training.

Bichons are highly capable of learning and they love to entertain. Even young Bichon puppies have an amazing capacity to learn. If you were able to make all your training sessions seem like fun and games you could probably teach your Bichon algebra! Well, maybe not quite algebra, but I think you get my message. Remember though, these young puppies also forget with great speed unless they are reminded of what they have learned by continual reinforcement.

Bichon Basics

What follows are the lessons every dog regardless of breed must learn. Your Bichon is no exception. He must learn to be a good canine citizen and once mastered, these Bichon Basics will allow him to do so.

Bichons are highly capable of learning and love to entertain. Once they realize their performances gain approval, they can be taught just about anything.

Leash Training

It is never too early to accustom your Bichon puppy to leash and collar. The properly fitting collar and the attached leash are your fail-safe way of keeping your Bichon under control. It is not necessary for your puppy or adult Bichon to wear a collar and identification tags when inside your home. However, he should never be outdoors in an unsecured area without collar and tags and the leash held securely in your hand.

It is best to begin getting your puppy accustomed to this new experience by leaving a soft collar around his neck for a few minutes at a time. Gradually extend the time you leave the collar on. Most Bichon puppies become accustomed to their collars very quickly and after a few scratches to remove it, forget they are even wearing one.

While you are playing with your puppy, attach a very lightweight leash to the collar. Don't try to guide him at first. The point is to accustom him to the feeling of having something hanging from the collar.

At first follow him wherever he goes while you hold the leash. After a bit, try and encourage him to follow you as you move away. Should he begin to balk a bit, coax him along with a treat of some kind. Hold the treat in front of his nose to encourage him to follow you. As soon as he takes a few steps toward you, praise him enthusiastically, give him a tiny bit of the treat, and continue to do so as you move slowly along.

Make the first lessons short, and remember—*f-u-n!* Continue the lessons at home or in the yard until your puppy is completely unconcerned about being on a leash. With a treat in one hand and the leash in the other you can begin to use both to guide him in the direction you wish to go. Begin your first walks in front of the house and eventually extend them down the street and eventually around the block. Try to encourage your puppy to walk on your left side. This will come in handy later.

The "Come" Command

The next most important lesson is for your Bichon puppy to come when called. Learning to come on command could save your puppy's life when the two of you venture out into the world. "Come" is the command all dogs must obey without question. The problem many owners create here is having their dog associate the "come" command with fear. They grow angry when their dog doesn't respond immediately to "come." When the dog finally does come or after a chase, the owner scolds the dog for not obeying. It shouldn't be hard to see why the dog begins to associate the word "come" with an unpleasant result.

Once your very young Bichon puppy has decided that you are the pack leader it is going to be very dependent upon you. There's no more "mom." You are tops in your

puppy's eyes. Your new little friend will want to stay as close to you as possible, especially in strange surroundings. When your puppy sees you moving away, his natural inclination will be to go right along with you. This is a perfect time to use the "come" command.

Later, as your puppy grows more self-confident and independent, you may want to attach a long leash or cord to the collar to insure getting the correct response. Again, *never chase or punish your puppy for not obeying the "come" command—* especially not in the initial stages of the lesson. It is very important that you praise your puppy and give a treat when he does come to you, even if he dawdles and takes his good old time to get to you.

The "Sit" and "Stay" Commands

Just as important to your Bichon's safety as the "No!" command and learning to come when called are the "Sit" and "Stay" commands. Most Bichon puppies learn the sit command easily, often in just a few minutes, especially if it appears to be a game and a food treat is involved. Your puppy should always be on collar and leash for the lessons. Young puppies are not beyond getting up and walking away when they have decided you and your lessons are boring.

Give the "Pierre, sit" command immediately before pushing down on his hindquarters or scooping his hind legs under him, molding him into a sit position. Praise him lavishly when he does sit, even though it is you who made it happen. Again, a food treat always seems to get the lesson across to the learning youngster.

Continue holding your puppy's rear end down and repeat the "sit" command several times. If your dog makes an attempt to get up, repeat the command yet again while exerting pressure on the rear end until the correct position is assumed. Make your Bichon stay in this position for increasing lengths of time. Begin with a few seconds and increase the

The properly fitting collar and the attached leash are your fail-safe way of keeping your Bichon under control. He should never be outdoors in an unsecured area without a collar and tags and the leash held securely in your hand.

time as lessons progress over the following weeks.

Don't test a very young puppy's patience to the limits. As bright as the Bichon breed is, remember you are dealing with a baby. The attention span of any youngster, canine or human, is relatively short.

The "Sit, Stay"

Depending on his age and once Pierre has mastered the "Sit" lesson, start working on the "Stay" command. With Pierre on leash and at your left side, give the "Pierre, sit" command. Put the palm of your right hand in front of his eyes and say *"Pierre, stay!"* Take a small step forward. If he attempts to get up to follow, firmly say, "Pierre, sit, stay!" While you are saying this, raise your hand, palm toward him, and again command "Pierre, stay!"

Any attempt on his part to get up must be corrected at once, returning him to the sit position, holding your palm up and repeating, "Pierre, stay!" Once he begins to understand what you want, gradually increase the distance you step back. With a long leash attached to his collar (here again, lightweight rope is fine) start with a few steps and gradually increase the distance to several yards.

As your Bichon masters this lesson and is able to remain in the sit position for as long as you dictate, avoid calling your dog *to you* at first. This makes the dog overly anxious to get up and run to you. Instead, walk back to your dog and say "OK"—a signal that the command is over. Later, when your Bichon becomes more reliable in this respect, you can call him to you.

It is best to keep the "Stay" part of the lesson to a minimum until the puppy is at least five or six months old. Everything in a very young Bichon's makeup urges it to stay close to you wherever you go. The puppy has bonded to you and forcing it to operate against its natural instincts can be bewildering.

Remember, in all these lessons you are dealing with a dog. Human strategy like sulking, arguing, blaming, threatening, and other tactics you might employ to get your way with other humans don't work with your dog! Dogs can learn to understand what your command means and they can learn to respond to it. However, they can't guess what all those subtle (and not so subtle) human poses mean.

The "Down" Command

Once your Bichon has mastered the "Sit" command and you are working on "Stay," you can begin work on the "Down" command. This is the one word command for lying down. Use the "Down" command *only* when you want your Bichon to lie down. If you want the puppy to get off your sofa or to stop jumping up on people, use the "Off" command. Don't interchange the two commands. Doing so serves only to confuse and will delay the response you want.

The "Down" position is especially useful if you want your Bichon to

Puppies learn the sit *command easily. Give the* sit *command immediately before pushing down on the dog's hindquarters or scooping his hind legs under him.*

remain in a particular place for an extended period of time. A dog is usually far more inclined to stay put when lying down than when sitting.

Teaching this command to some Bichons may take a little more time and patience than some of the other lessons. If you think back on what you were told about a dog's body language, you will remember that the down position represents submissiveness to the dog. Dogs that are inclined to be more independent therefore may take additional time to develop any enthusiasm for the "Down" lesson.

Kneel in front of your Bichon with the dog facing you. Hold a treat in your right hand with the excess part of the leash in your left hand. Hold the treat under the puppy's nose and slowly bring your hand down to the ground. Your dog will follow the treat with his head and neck. As he does, give the *"Down"* command and exert *light* pressure on his shoulders with your left hand. If he resists the pressure *do not continue pushing down.* Doing so will only create more resistance. Better to slide his front legs out from under him and toward yourself.

An alternative method of getting your Bichon headed into the down position is to move around and kneel at his right side. As you draw

An easy way of getting your Bichon into the down position is to move around and kneel at his right side. As you draw his attention downward with a treat in your right hand, slide your left hand under his front legs and gently slide his legs forward.

his attention downward with the treat in your right hand, slide your left hand under his front legs and gently slide them forward.

As Pierre's forelegs begin to slide out to his front, keep moving the treat along the ground until his whole body is lying on the ground. Continually repeat "Pierre, down!" while this is going on. Once he has assumed the position you desire, give him the treat and a lot of praise. But if he should attempt to get up, repeat the "Down" command and assist back into position. Be firm and patient and eventually your Bichon will master the lesson and begin to think of it as another fun game.

The "Long Down"

In teaching your Bichon the "Long Down" you will follow the same basic procedure you used in working on the long sit. With your dog on leash and at your left side, give the "Pierre, down" command. Put the palm of your right hand in front of his eyes and say *"Pierre, stay!"* Take a small step forward. If he attempts to get up to follow, firmly say, "Pierre, down," and then "Pierre, stay!" While you are saying this raise your hand, palm toward the dog, and again command "Pierre, stay!"

Once your Bichon begins to understand what you want, you can gradually increase the distance you step back. Use the same long leash you used for the "Sit, Stay" exercise, starting with a few steps back and gradually increasing the distance to several yards.

The "Heel" Lesson

No doubt you've seen other dog owners in almost horizontal position racing down the street behind their dog. Either that or they are trying to disentangle their legs from a leash while their dog lunges right, left, and every which way but forward. Granted a Bichon is not large enough to pull your arm out of its socket, but you'll admit it's much more enjoyable to walk with a dog trained to walk calmly beside you.

You can assist the implementation of this lesson early on—in the early stages of leash training. When you take your puppy for a walk, get him accustomed to walking on your left side. If he drifts off to your right, shorten the leash and guide him back to your left and say "Good boy, Pierre."

If you are going to pursue any kind of obedience training in the future, all training is done from the left side. Having to change sides later will only serve to confuse the dog.

A finely made chain-link training collar is very useful for your leash lessons. It provides both quick pressure around the neck and a snapping sound, both of which get the dog's attention. Some people refer to this as a "choke collar." Fear not, the chain-link collar used properly does not choke a dog. The pet emporium from which you purchase the collar will be able to show you the proper way to put this collar on your dog.

As you walk with your Bichon, the leash should cross your body from the dog's collar to your right hand.

Putting on the Chain-Link Collar

The chain-link collar has a ring at each end. Hold a ring in each hand and loop the chain down through the opposite ring. Pull the chain up slightly with your right hand and lay the collar down on a flat surface. If you separate the top part of the loop it will form a letter "P." Facing your dog, with the collar in this form, slip the collar over his head. The free ring at the bottom of the "P" is the ring to which you will attach your leash. Do not put the collar on so that the "P" formation is facing in the opposite direction, as it will not have the freedom to tighten and release as easily as it would if put on properly.

The excess portion of the leash will be folded into your right hand, and your left hand will then be free on the leash to make corrections. Keep the leash slack and tighten it only to give a quick snap to get your dog back in position.

A quick short jerk on the leash with your left hand will keep your dog from lunging side to side, pulling ahead, or lagging back. As you make a correction, give the "Heel" command with the dog's name. Keep the leash slack as long as your dog maintains the proper position alongside your left leg.

If your dog begins to drift away, give the leash a sharp snap and guide your pupil back to left side. Do

When you start taking walks with your Bichon, accustom him to walking on your left side. This will begin his introduction to the **heel** *command, where he will learn to walk at your left with his shoulder next to your leg.*

not pull on the lead with steady pressure. What is needed is a sharp jerking motion to get your dog's attention. I've heard obedience trainers tell students that "success in training will be in direct proportion to the jerk at the end of the lead." Everyone in the class usually doubles up with laughter at this point, but it is a point well made. Eventually your puppy will automatically go to your left side as you walk along.

In learning to heel, your Bichon will walk on your left side with his shoulder next to your leg no matter which direction you might go or how quickly you turn. With your left arm

hanging down, the fingers of your left hand should be directly above your dog's shoulder. If you have to swing your arm out or bend your fingers back, your dog is not in the right place. (For those of you who have short fingers, *imagine* you are doing this!)

Begin with your Bichon sitting at your left side with his shoulder next to your leg. Step forward on your right foot, and as you step forward give the "Pierre, heel!" command. The leash should be slack. Once you start off, Pierre will probably move out with you. If he attempts to pull away in any direction, give the sharp jerk and command "Pierre, heel." Do not keep the leash taut and attempt to pull the dog back into position—use a clean quick snap of the leash.

If your Bichon is frightened or intimidated by the exercise, do not administer the jerk. Coax the dog into position and try to make obeying a fun game and worthy of a treat when done well. If your Bichon is still extremely intimidated, there are cloth training collars that eliminate the snapping sound, but I assure you they do not work as well.

Training Classes

As mentioned previously, there are few limits to what a patient, consistent owner can teach a Bichon. For the advanced basic obedience course and for work beyond that, it is wise to consider local professional assistance.

Qualified professional trainers have had long experience in avoiding the pitfalls of obedience training and can help you to avoid these mistakes as well. Even Bichon owners who have never trained a dog before have found, with professional assistance, that their dog has become a superstar in obedience circles.

This training assistance can be obtained in many ways. Classes are particularly important for your Bichon's socialization and concentration. Most Bichons look at every new dog and every new person as potential playmates. This is all well and good, but at the same time Bichons deal with these meetings with such exuberance, it is important that your Bichon learns to respond obediently regardless of surrounding conditions.

At many parks and recreation facilities there are free-of-charge classes sponsored by various organizations. Very formal and sometimes expensive individual lessons with private trainers are also available in most cities.

A Bichon can and will learn with any good professional. However, unless your schedule gives you no time at all to train your own dog, having someone else do the training for you would be last on my list of recommendations. The rapport that develops between an owner who has trained his or her own Bichon to be a pleasant companion and good canine citizen is very special—well worth the time and patience it requires to achieve.

Finding a Good Trainer

If you decide to seek the help of a dog trainer, the number of them available will probably overwhelm you. Take promises of overnight success with a grain of salt. Smart as our Bichons are, good trainers take as much time with each dog as is necessary and no two dogs absorb the training at the same rate of speed. Good dog training is about training your dog well, not how fast the dog completes the course.

Don't misunderstand what a dog trainer's real purpose is. The ideal trainer is one who is experienced at teaching you to train your dog. The fact that an outsider is able to have Pierre behave like a perfect gentleman will have no effect upon his behavior at home if you are not equipped to enforce the rules.

Citizen Bichon

The rewards of owning this great breed are practically limitless, but to gain access to what has earned Bichons their great reputation, you must provide the framework from which your dog will reliably operate. The following is a checklist that all Bichon owners should consider a basic part of their dog's education.

• Walk on leash quietly at your side even on a crowded street.
• Allow any stranger to pet your dog when you give the OK.
• Come immediately when called.

The good looks of this well-cared for Bichon Frise have great appeal but it is the owner's responsibility to make sure that the attractive picture is backed up with training that will make him a good canine citizen.

• Sit and lie down on command and remain in position until you give the come command.

• Be tolerant of other dogs and pets.

These are things that every companion Bichon must be taught and must consider the everyday way of behaving. Your Bichon is more than capable of mastering all of the items on this checklist; it is up to you to make sure your dog is given the opportunity to do so.

Chapter Ten

Together Wherever You Go

What is so wonderful about owning a Bichon Frise is that not only is it able to provide a lifetime of fun and companionship within your home, there's an entire world of fascinating things you or your entire family can share beyond your front door.

Many new owners of well-bred Bichons discover the wonderful world of conformation dog shows and become avidly involved. There are a host of other fun pursuits that both Bichon and owner enjoy so much they have become all but addicted. Because Bichons are such clowns and naturals in the world of entertainment there are activities that suit their abilities to run, jump, dance, and strut with the best of the canine world.

So you and your Bichon can share your lives at home or away. Let's take a look at just a few of the activities that you and your Bichon might enjoy.

In the United States the American Kennel Club and the United Kennel Club sponsor many kinds of competitive events in which all registered purebred dogs may compete. The events run the gamut from the more formal conformation judging (that event you watch on TV from New York each year) through to the exciting and fun agility trials and the equally crowd- and dog-pleasing flyball.

Conformation Shows

Currently the most popular and well-attended dog events are conformation shows, and competition is always very keen in the Bichon ring. Conformation dog shows take place nearly every weekend of the year in one part of the country or another and are open to all nonneutered AKC or UKC registered dogs.

Generally speaking, conformation shows fall into two major categories: match shows and championship events. Match shows are primarily for puppies or inexperienced dogs that are not ready to compete for championship points. In most cases classes are offered for dogs from about three months of age and older.

Championship shows provide a great competitive outlet for both dog and owner. The Bichon Frise is very often found in the Winners Circle of the country's largest all-breed shows.

How Dogs Are Judged

Classes: In every breed, dogs (Males) are judged first, then bitches (Females). For each sex there are six classes:

1. Puppy—for dogs between 6 months and under one year of age;

2. 12 Months & Under 18—for dogs between 12 months and under 18 months of age;

3. Novice—for dogs which have never won a first prize;

4. Bred by Exhibitor—for dogs except Champions, six months of age and over, which shall be presently owned and exhibited by the same person or kennel who were the recognized breeders on the records of the American Kennel Club;

5. American Bred—for dogs born in the U.S.A.;

6. Open—for all dogs American and foreign bred.

Usually the most experienced show dogs are to be seen in the American Bred and Open Classes.

Winners: Into this competition come the first prize winners of the above classes, and two awards are made: Winners (purple ribbon) and Reserve Winners (purple and white ribbon).

Best of Breed Competition:
Dogs of either sex which are already Champions and the two which were chosen Winners compete here and one is chosen Best of Breed. This dog competes later in the Groups as sole representative of his breed.

Best of Winners: Only two dogs compete in this class—the Winners Dog and the Winners Bitch. One is chosen Best of Winners.

Championship Points: Championship points can be won by one dog and one bitch in each breed. The Winners Dog and Winners Bitch receive these points. The number of points depends on the number of each sex competing in each breed. When a dog has received 15 points he is a Champion and holds the title all his life.

What a Judge Judges on: As a judge goes over each dog in the ring he is comparing him to a mental picture of the perfect dog of that breed. He judges each dog on:

1. Physical structure (head, teeth, feet, bone structure, muscle tone, etc.)

2. Condition (proper weight, condition of coat, animation, etc.)

3. Gait—as seen from front, side, and rear.

4. Temperament—penalizing heavily for shyness or viciousness.

The End of the Show: In a dog show the competition becomes keener and more exciting at the end. When all breeds have been judged, only one dog in each breed remains undefeated—the one which was chosen Best of Breed. These dogs are called to compete in one of the seven groups—Sporting, Hound, Working, Terrier, Toy, Non-Sporting, and Herding. One wins each group. These seven Group Winners meet in the final competition and one is chosen.

Best in Show: This dog stands alone at the end of the show, remaining undefeated.

Match Shows

Matches are the perfect place for you and your Bichon to learn what dog shows are about. These match shows are far more informal than the championship shows. Since they are more casual there is plenty of time for the beginning handler to make mistakes along with everyone else and to ask questions and seek assistance from more experienced exhibitors or from the officiating judges. Information regarding these matches can sometimes be found in the classified sections of Sunday newspapers under "Dogs for Sale."

Matches can be entered on the day of the show. Most clubs accept entries at the show site on the morning of the event. The person taking your entry will be able to help you fill out the form and give you the needed preliminary instructions. All the information required is on your

Bichon's registration certificate, so you might want to take a copy of that with you.

Championship Shows

Championship shows are a lot more formal, so I suggest your considering entering these events after you've gained experience by showing in a few of the match shows. How these events are judged is outlined in the accompanying chart, "How Dogs Are Judged."

Championship shows are sponsored by various all-breed kennel clubs or by a club specializing in one breed of dog. Both the AKC and UKC can provide you with the name of the all-breed kennel club in your area, and the Bichon Frise Club of America can let you know if there is a local Bichon club in your area.

The Road to the Title

For a dog registered with the American Kennel Club to become a champion, it must be awarded a total of 15 championship points. These points are awarded to the best male and best female non-champions in each breed. The number of championship points that can be won at a particular show is based on the number of entries in a dog's own breed and sex competing at the show. Of the 15 points required, two of the wins must be what are called "majors" (i.e., three or more points). These two majors have to be won under two different judges.

The UKC championship process is very similar to that of the AKC, but in most cases it takes fewer dogs to achieve the title. Details on UKC championships can be obtained on the organization's Web site.

Catalogs sold at championship shows list all the particulars relevant to every dog entered in the show, like name, owner, breeder, and the dog's sire and dam. The catalog also lists the number of dogs required in each breed to win from one through five points.

How to Enter a Championship Show

All clubs sponsoring an American Kennel Club championship show must issue what is called a premium list. A premium list contains all the information you will need in order to enter that club's show. These premium lists are sent out by professional show superintendents several weeks in advance of the closing date for entries for that show.

You must advise the show superintendent in your area that you wish to receive all premium lists for shows that will be held in your area. A list of show superintendents can be obtained from the American Kennel Club. Once your name is entered on a show superintendent's list you will continue to receive premium lists for all shows staged by that organization as long as you continue to show your dog.

The premium list will give you the date, location, and closing date for entries for a particular show. It will also list the entry fee, the judges for each of the breeds eligible to com-

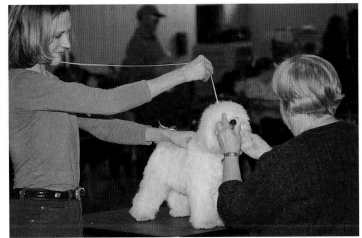

In the show ring, the Bichon is posed for examination on a table. It is extremely important that your dog not be apprehensive when the judge approaches.

pete at the show, and the prizes that will be awarded in each breed.

Included in the premium list is the entry form you will need to complete to enter the show. All of the information you need to complete the entry form appears on your dog's American Kennel Club registration certificate. The information you enter on this form will appear in the catalog on the day of the show.

Classes of Competition

The premium list also shows the classes in which you can enter your Bichon at American Kennel Club shows. Read the information in the premium list carefully. Often there are lower rates for puppy classes as well as other exceptions you should be aware of.

Note that in dog show terminology males are referred to as "dogs" and females as "bitches." It is required that you include the sex of your Bichon on the entry blank so

that your Bichon is not put into the incorrect class. It is also important to remember that while at the show, only the males are "dogs" and your loved and adored Ami will have to be referred to as a "bitch." Your entry will be called to the ring in that way.

How the day progresses from beginning to end can be better understood by studying the accompanying "Dog Show Judging Procedure" chart. The chart shows how a dog might progress from the first class of the day through to Best In Show that evening.

Professional handlers offer their services to those who do not wish to handle their own dog at a show or who are unable to do so. These professionals can be contacted at most dog shows. When they have completed their work for the day they are happy to discuss the possibility and the practicality of having your Bichon professionally handled.

DOG SHOW JUDGING PROCEDURE

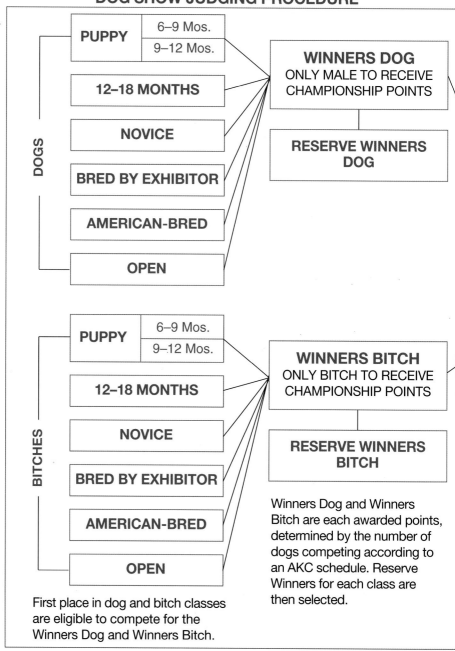

DOGS

| PUPPY | 6–9 Mos. |
| | 9–12 Mos. |

12–18 MONTHS

NOVICE

BRED BY EXHIBITOR

AMERICAN-BRED

OPEN

WINNERS DOG
ONLY MALE TO RECEIVE CHAMPIONSHIP POINTS

RESERVE WINNERS DOG

BITCHES

| PUPPY | 6–9 Mos. |
| | 9–12 Mos. |

12–18 MONTHS

NOVICE

BRED BY EXHIBITOR

AMERICAN-BRED

OPEN

WINNERS BITCH
ONLY BITCH TO RECEIVE CHAMPIONSHIP POINTS

RESERVE WINNERS BITCH

Winners Dog and Winners Bitch are each awarded points, determined by the number of dogs competing according to an AKC schedule. Reserve Winners for each class are then selected.

First place in dog and bitch classes are eligible to compete for the Winners Dog and Winners Bitch.

BEST OF BREED or VARIETY COMPETITION consists of both male and female champions, plus Winners Dog and Winners Bitch. Best of Breed or Variety Award qualifies this dog to represent its Breed in its own group.

SPORTING GROUP

HOUND GROUP

WORKING GROUP

TERRIER GROUP

BEST IN SHOW

This Dog stands alone at the end of the Show, remaining undefeated.

BEST OF BREED COMPETITION

TOY GROUP

BEST OF WINNERS

NON-SPORTING GROUP

BEST OF OPPOSITE SEX

HERDING GROUP

BEST OF WINNERS is selected from the Winners Dog and Winners Bitch.

BEST OF OPPOSITE SEX is then selected from the remaining dogs of the Opposite Sex to the Best of Breed/Variety.

FIRST PLACE WINNER in each of the Seven Groups represents its Group for Best In Show.

Showing Your Own Bichon

The foregoing explains the kinds of shows you can enter and how to go about doing so. However, getting ready for a dog show begins long before you actually walk into the ring at a championship show. This is particularly so of Bichons because coat preparation and grooming are a very important part of developing the winning look. Chapter 7, "The Crowning Glory," will give you some idea of the expertise required in this area.

Beginners have a great deal to learn. At first it seems overwhelming but, keep in mind that everyone was once a novice. No matter how the pros perform, understand they did not know how to do all that when they entered their first show.

Much of what you need to know is contained in books and magazine articles. Read all you can. Attend dog shows and observe the people in the ring who are winning with their Bichons. You will quickly see how much skilled handling enhances a dog's looks and its chances of winning.

The important thing is to begin to master the art of handling your own Bichon. This can begin as soon as you bring your puppy home. Teaching your puppy to stand still while it is being brushed is the initial phase of learning the proper stance in the show ring.

The judge examines Bichons while the dog is posed on a table. It is bottom-line important that your Bichon not be apprehensive when the judge attempts to examine it.

You can practice staging this at home whenever strangers stop by. If your Bichon is going to be a show dog, the more strangers who are allowed to put their hands on your dog, the better. The dog must be completely at ease when the judge does the examination. Any attempt on the dog's part to back away or, worse yet, snap at the judge will diminish your chances. In the case of biting or even attempting to bite — your dog will be dealt with by dismissing you both from the ring immediately and permanently until you take steps for reinstatement.

Showing dogs is an enjoyable hobby, but it takes hard work and a lot of study and practice to master both the grooming techniques and the art of handling your dog well. Patience and practice will help make you proficient. You will not become expert overnight.

Junior Showmanship

Junior Showmanship is for all youngsters who are at least 10 years old and no older than 16. This fun activity for the junior set teaches good sportsmanship, responsibility, and the fun of competition.

Juniors are judged entirely on their ability and skill in presenting their dog. The judge does not consider the dog's conformation. Classes are divided by the junior handler's age and prior accomplishment.

The booklet *Regulations for Junior Showmanship* published by the American Kennel Club contains all the regulations pertaining to this event and may be obtained directly from that organization.

Games and Sports

Flyball

Flyball is certainly one of the most exciting activities you and your Bichon can choose from the breed's long list of fun things to do. The degree to which Ami and Pierre are obsessed with their tennis balls will determine in good part how successful they might be as participants in this event.

In flyball the dogs are organized into four teams. The team races on a relay system. At the signal, each dog must clear four hurdles, release a ball from the flyball box, catch it in the air, and return with the ball to the starting point so that the next teammate can start off. The team is racing against the clock, and the speed and excitement make for a very enthusiastic ringside.

Three titles can be earned: Flyball Dog (F.D.), Flyball Dog Excellent (F.D.X.) and Flyball Dog Champion (F.D.Ch.). Information regarding rules, training, and where events are held can be obtained directly from the North American Flyball Association, Inc. (See Useful Addresses and Literature for address.)

Freestyle

Freestyle is a relatively new canine sport, with one paw in obedi-

Junior Showmanship is a competitive event open to youngsters from 10 to 16 years of age. It is a fun activity for the junior set that also teaches good sportsmanship.

ence and the other in dance and/or calisthenics. Many of the basic obedience exercises are called upon, but in Freestyle there are many more movements required of the dog and handler in a routine set to music.

Teamwork and coordination are prime factors in this event. Scoring is based on the performance of both dog and handler. Execution of some of the standard obedience movements is required, but nonstandard movements that the dogs are called upon to perform also weigh heavily. Enthusiasm, degree of difficulty of the movements displayed, and

Agility competition might easily be called "Canine Olympics" in that it calls for both speed and agility. The dog completing a given obstacle course in the shortest time wins. It is a fun event for the dogs, their owners, and the spectators who cheer their favorites on.

appropriateness of music and its interpretation are additional scoring factors.

Frisbee

Not all dogs are wild about playing Frisbee. However, if Ami or Pierre decide catching that plastic disc while it flies through the air is a jolly good time, it could become an obsession. Some Bichons will take to catching and retrieving a Frisbee at their first try and get better with each catch. Other Bichons need to develop a liking for the object first. One of the easiest ways to do this is to initially use the Frisbee as a food dish.

There are local, regional, national, and international Frisbee competitions, and prizes range from a cou-ple of hundred dollars into the thousands. There are even international Frisbee teams that meet annually for the World Cup!

Agility

Agility competition is for all intents and purposes an obstacle course for dogs. Everyone involved (and everyone who watches) appears to be having a great time, and the sport has become outrageously popular at dog shows and fairs throughout the world. There are tunnels, cat walks,

Ten Parts of the Good Citizen Test

1. Appearance and grooming. The dog must be clean and appear to be free of parasites.

2. Acceptance of a friendly stranger. The dog is required to allow a friendly stranger to approach and speak to the handler.

3. Walking on a loose leash. The dog has to walk along attentively next to the handler.

4. Walking through a crowd. The dog is required to walk along paying attention to the handler without interfering with other people or dogs.

5. Sit and Down on command and Staying in place. The dog has to respond to each of the handler's commands.

6. Come when called. After being put in a sit or lie down position ten feet away, the dog must return to the handler when called.

7. Sit while touched by a stranger. A friendly stranger must be able to pet the dog.

8. Positive reaction to another dog. The dog has to keep its attention on the handler even in the presence of another dog.

9. Calm reaction to distracting sights or noises. These distractions can be an unusual or loud noise or sight of a bicycle or unusual looking object.

10. Supervised separation. The dog must wait calmly while tied with leash while owner is out of sight for three minutes.

Anyone interested in this program can obtain information regarding rules as well as when and where testing is held directly from the American Kennel Club in North Carolina.

seesaws, and numerous other obstacles that the canine contestants have to master off leash while they are being timed.

The idea began in England and caught the public's attention when it was first presented at the world-famed Crufts Dog Show in London in 1978. By 1986 it was already a major event in Great Britain and had caught on so well in the United States that the United States Dog Agility Association (USDAA) was organized in 1986.

Canine Good Citizen Program

There is no doubt that the vast majority of the Bichons owned around the world serve the same purpose—to be a pleasant addition to their owner's lives—nothing more, nothing less. One of the best ways Bichons can fulfill that role is to be relied upon to behave acceptably when they venture into the world at large. One of the best ways I know of insuring this is giving your Bichon the

Obedience competition is precise and based completely on how well a dog performs a set series of exercises. The exercise levels include basics like sit, lie down, *and* heel *to the advanced scent discrimination and directed jumping.*

opportunity to learn the basics of the Canine Good Citizen Program (CGC).

The purpose of this program and its ultimate test is to demonstrate that the canine enrolled is well-mannered and an asset to the community. This isn't a competition of any kind; a dog is scored completely on its ability to master the basic requirements for a well-behaved dog. There are ten parts to the test (see page 101) and the dog must pass all ten in order to be awarded the CGC certificate.

Obedience Trials

The Canine Good Citizen program gives you only an inkling of what your Bichon is capable of learning. The breed is particularly adept at learning what is offered in the world of Obedience trials. Obedience trials are held at both championship shows and at matches. The same informal entry procedures that apply to conformation matches apply here as well. The championship or "sanctioned" obedience trials are normally held in conjunction with conformation shows and they also require pre-entry. They are handled in a much more formal manner.

Obedience classes are definitely prerequisites here. Obedience competition is highly precise and based completely on how well your dog performs a set series of exercises. The exercises required in the various classes of competition range from the basics like heel, sit, and lie down in the Novice class on through the sophisticated exercises of the Utility and Tracking Dog levels that require scent discrimination and directed jumping.

Each level has a degree that can be earned after attaining qualifying scores at a given number of shows. The competition levels and corresponding degrees are: Novice, earning a Companion Dog degree (CD),

Open, which earns the Companion Dog Excellent degree (CDX), Utility, earning the Utility Dog and Utility Dog Excellent degrees (UD and UDX). Tracking events earn the rare Tracking Dog and Tracking Dog Excellent titles (TD and TDX).

Undoubtedly because of their trick and circus dog heritage, Bichons have proven to be excellent candidates for obedience titles. Many have achieved their Companion Dog and Companion Dog Excellent degrees, and the breed is proud to claim titleholders in even the most demanding of the categories.

Therapy Dogs

You'll be amazed at the warm feeling you'll come away with when you and your Bichon have spent the day bringing a little sunshine into some lives that otherwise could be quite dreary. Children and elderly people especially seem to light up when they are visited by dogs and are amazed how sweet and attentive a Bichon can be.

Medical journals continually substantiate the great therapeutic value to the patients who come in contact with trained therapy dogs. Stress reduction and lowered blood pressure are proven to be a direct result of these human-to-animal associations. And what you'll get out of it is beyond measure; trust me.

Two organizations—the Delta Society and Therapy Dogs International—test and register Bichons and other breeds that are temperamentally suitable to visit hospitals and homes for the aged.

Dog Clubs

If you plan to participate in any of the many dog activities listed here or those you find on your own, you are well on your way to becoming what is referred to in dog game vernacular as a real "dyed-in-the-wool dog person." You'll find a host of comrades in the dog clubs that abound throughout the country.

There are all-breed clubs and specialty clubs for just about every field of doggy endeavor you've decided to pursue. The members of these clubs can assist you in your progress and I can assure you the clubs themselves are always looking for members who are able to assist them in the cause.

Most have membership requirements and a code of ethics their members must abide by; these caveats are intended for the good of the breed and protection of the existing membership. Peruse the list of resources under Useful Addresses and Literature for organizations that can help you become proficient in your area of interest and that you can help to keep that avocation thriving.

Chapter Eleven

On the Road

Travel with your Bichon includes every journey—from trips to the corner store to drives across the country. Certain considerations apply no matter how short or long the trip—number one is safety.

Even if you decide your pal will have to stay behind, there are questions to be answered if there isn't someone at home to take over. Where will your Bichon stay while you are gone? Will Ami wither away if abandoned to a boarding kennel? Can you check a boarding kennel's reputation before you trust Pierre to care there?

Perhaps a pet sitter is a better answer? Is there anyone experienced and reliable who is willing to come in several times daily to check on your Bichon? Would you prefer to have someone stay in your home as a sitter while you're gone?

Sooner or later, every dog owner I've known, married or single, family person or not, has had to answer all these questions. Waiting until the last minute to get the answers for these questions could provide unnecessary headaches and confusion.

Safety First

Let's start with the precautions that apply regardless of the length of your trip. There are a number of things you must think seriously about. Two of the most important are temperature and the length of time required for the stops you will be making.

Time and Temperature

Today most cars are equipped with air-conditioning. It can be very warm outdoors, but if you and your dog are traveling in an air-conditioned car or van, that won't make a lot of difference. That is, if you don't plan to stop.

Most of us don't think of temperatures in the mid 80s as unbearable. In fact, if you were lounging on the chaise in the shade, you might consider that ideal. On a sunny day inside a car, even with windows partially rolled down, that same temperature can soar to over 100 degrees in just a few minutes and over 120 degrees in not much more than 20 minutes. Your Bichon is not able to withstand these temperatures without suffering permanent brain damage or death. *Do not take chances with your dog in a car on warm days!*

If there are stops planned in even moderately warm weather, think ahead and ask yourself whether your Bichon will be able to accompany you indoors or to a shaded spot. Most office buildings, department stores, and restaurants exclude dogs other than those used in guiding the blind or assisting their handicapped owners. Many parking lots of these buildings offer little or no shade.

Leaving car windows down helps little on a hot day. Sun shining through the front and rear windows sends temperatures up and the metal of the vehicle seems to trap the heat inside. The safest rule on a hot day is never leave your pet in a vehicle unless the vehicle can be parked in a completely shaded area and you can leave the windows rolled down.

Nowadays, there are few places where a driver would be inclined to leave a car open to the first thief that comes along. If you do leave the windows down you must keep the vehicle in view at all times. Don't even consider it at all if your Bichon isn't safely installed in a shipping kennel or cage.

Regardless of how well trained your Bichon is, if it gets too hot inside the car, good sense is going to make the dog try to escape. My advice: if it's very hot and you know you will have to make prolonged stops and are not sure of available

Most Bichons are excellent travelers, but it is the owner's responsibility to set acceptable behavior and take measures to assure the dog's safety in the car.

shade—*leave your dog at home in a cool room!*

Fasten Those Seat Belts!

It might be nice to have Pierre loose right next to you so he can view the passing scenery, but he can be injured or killed instantly by being thrown against the windshield if you make a sudden stop or there is a collision. Then too, if he were to spot something of great interest through the window on your side of the car, he could interfere with your controls and cause an accident.

All the reasons for our buckling our seat belts when we drive apply to our pets as well. Canine seat belts are now available that can be adapted to almost any make of car and size of dog. This provides both the safety and restraint that can assure both you and your pet a comfortable and safe trip.

Actually your Bichon is safest properly confined to the rear seat of a passenger car. The barriers that are provided to confine dogs to the rear section of a station wagon or van do nothing to protect a breed as small as a Bichon. Being thrown up against the barriers can be just as dangerous as being thrown against a window.

Whether with seat belts or in a crate, all dogs should be restrained for safety's sake. Even if riding in a solid crate robs Ami or Pierre of their opportunity to see all the sights, better that than being hurled out of the back seat or along the full length of a van.

Vacations and Extended Travel

Identification and Medication

Most states throughout the country, as well as travel to Canada and Mexico, will require up-to-date vaccination against rabies. Crossing the border to Canada and Mexico will also require health certificates validated by your veterinarian. Be sure your dog's rabies inoculations are current and that your Bichon is wearing the certifying tag your veterinarian will issue.

Your veterinarian will also be able to advise you on any special needed precautions in the area of your destination. In certain sections of the country there is risk of tick-borne Lyme disease and heartworm.

The Bichon Suitcase

If you plan ahead, even the longest trip with your Bichon can be a totally pleasant experience. Think about your doggie "musts" at home and that will help create your list for travel.

People who show their dogs are on the road a good part of every month, and experience has taught them to carry *everything* their dogs might need both for daily routine and in an emergency. Your traveling companion probably has no need for all the cosmetic equipment that a show dog might require, but there are a number of doggie items that should definitely be stowed in your Bichon's steamer trunk:
• Regular drinking water in gallon plastic containers
• Sufficient food for length of trip plus a bit more. Changing food suddenly can cause diarrhea.
• Brush, comb, and grooming supplies
• Leash, collar with clearly marked I.D. and rabies tags
• First aid kit
• Solid or collapsible crate
• List of parks and/or rest stops along the way

- Poop scooper and plastic grocery bags
- Appropriate bedding for season of the year
- Food and water dishes
- Favorite toys
- Current medications, including flea and tick controls and heartworm medications
- Paper and terry towels for clean up and drying
- Ice chest with refreezable "blue ice" packs. Wonderful cool-down when wrapped in a towel and placed at bottom of the travel crate in extremely hot weather.

Holidog Inns

Another good reason for a travel crate is that it provides a place for your Bichon if your trip has an overnight or longer stay at its destination. If your hosts also have a dog, having a crate for your Bichon will prove to be a godsend. Most dogs are not particularly happy about another pooch invading their home territory, and some can be hostile about the situation. Thinking they'll work it out between themselves might work just fine for your dog but don't rely upon your host's dog being as hospitable as his owner.

Not all hotels and motels accept dogs. Some people stop over along the way only when they grow tired of driving—the hotel that is nearest to that point gets their business. This will probably not work when traveling with your Bichon. Driving until you are totally exhausted and then starting a search for dog-friendly accommodations may be an option, but it isn't a very attractive one.

Those who find their traveling more relaxed when they know that they do have accommodations at a specific location will do best to speak directly to the hotel or motel beforehand. Many of these establishments require additional fees for pets in the rooms or refundable deposits if there is no damage. Some establishments advertise that they do accept dogs, but this may mean that all dogs must be confined outside the rooms in their own travel crates.

Air Travel

If after reading the preceding you think that flying with Pierre might simplify matters, think again. Air travel has as many burdensome considerations plus a whole set of additional hoops for you and your traveling buddy to jump through.

Air travel isn't impossible, but I can assure you it is no way as easy as having your Bichon safely secured in the back of your vehicle. The fact that Bichons will fit under the seat in front of an airline passenger eliminates some of the headaches, but even then, prior (as in *prior!*) planning is essential.

Most airlines will allow you to carry your Bichon on board as long as it is safely secured in a canine travel container. That container must fit under the seat in front of you and is considered one of the two bags you are allowed to carry on board.

The total number of dogs that may be transported on any flight in that manner is restricted—usually from one to three per flight. Some airlines allow you to reserve this arrangement in advance, others operate on a first come-first served basis. Make sure you check in advance regarding these specifications.

There is an additional charge for this service—usually around $80 or more each way. You may wonder why airlines charge an additional fee to put a dog rather than any other

Doggie Travel Brochures

The Automobile Association of America publishes annually updated catalogs listing accommodations throughout the nation and most indicate whether they accept dogs. Dawbert Press also publishes a series of dog-friendly travel guides written by Dawn and Robert Habgood called *On the Road Again with Man's Best Friend*. The local chamber of commerce in many cities can be very helpful in providing a list of hotels and motels that accept dogs and may also be able to provide a list of local veterinarians. Veterinary hospitals are usually aware of which local accommodations will accept dogs and it certainly is prudent to have quick reference to a veterinarian anyway.

travel bag under the seat in front of you. The best answer I've been able to find is because they can.

If not on board, your Bichon must fly as excess baggage in the cargo hold of the plane. The cost for this continually increases, so it is hard to give a ballpark figure, but conservatively you should plan on at least $100 each way.

Air travel for dogs is no longer unique; hundreds of dogs accompany their owners back and forth across the country each day. The Department of Agriculture estimates that approximately 600,000 animals a year travel by air. A good percentage of that number is made up of dogs and cats.

Obviously, air travel for pets is not entirely risk free. Whenever travel by air is necessary there are a number of safety measures to increase the odds of a safe arrival for your Bichon:

1. Always call the airline of your choice. Check out their policies regarding shipping dogs. Select the airline that offers the greatest safety assurances.

2. Make sure you understand the rules. There are all kinds of rules and regulations governing what kind of crate the individual airlines accept, how the crate should be identified and where delivery and pick up must take place. Well ahead of your departure date make sure you understand *exactly* what you must do in order to comply.

3. Advance reservations are a must! Airlines will accept only a given number of dogs per flight whether on board or in cargo. The airline agent or your travel agent will be able to reserve your dog's flight when you make your own reservation. I strongly recommend that you confirm (and then reconfirm) before your flight departure date.

4. Schedule direct, nonstop flights whenever possible. Connecting flights and long stopovers increase the risk of loss and fatalities. Overnight ("red-eye") and first flights out in the morning are the least crowded and offer better temperatures.

5. Talk to your veterinarian. Many states require a health certificate signed by a veterinarian and nearly all airlines will require one whether your destination requires one or not. Take the advice of your veterinarian, who knows your dog and may have suggestions to make. Discuss the need, if any, for tranquilizing your Bichon before shipping.

6. "Airline approved" shipping crates. The crate or kennel you ship your dog in must be "airline approved" or one that is purchased directly from the airline. ATA regulations state "the shipping crate must be large enough for your dog to stand up and turn around in."

This may require some discussion and diplomacy on your part. Some shipping clerks interpret the ATA's regulation to mean the crate should be large enough to raise a family in! "Just enough" room protects your dog from being thrown around should turbulent weather occur in

Is Air Travel Safe for Your Pet?

The Air Transport Association (ATA) reports that 99 percent of all animals shipped in the United States reach their destination "without incident." Of course that remaining 1 percent of reported "incidents" includes everything from minor complaints to the death of the animal. Since dogs travel in the cargo area of the plane it should be understood that while this area is pressurized there are no air-conditioning or heat controls. Because of this, the Federal regulations require that no animal be shipped by air if the ground temperature at either end of the flight is above 85 degrees or below 45 degrees.

flight. A crate that is too large makes it easy for a dog to be thrown from side to side.

Crate preparation. Federal law requires absorbent bedding be placed on the bottom of the crate. You must also supply food and water in dishes that are attached to the inside of the crate's wire door. Tape a small bag of food to the top of the crate. Tape a sign to the top of the crate giving instructions for food and water for the next 24 hours in case of delays. You are not allowed to put a lock on the crate door, but you can increase security with bungee cords or tape.

Crate markings. The airline will supply you with a "Live Animal"

With some advance planning, you can take your Bichon with you on a vacation trip. If you have done your homework, you will both enjoy the change of pace.

sticker at the point of departure. This must be securely and visibly attached to the outside of the crate. Tape a label giving full information regarding contact persons at point of departure and destination. Carefully indicate both phone numbers and addresses.

7. Collar and I.D. tags. Regardless of how careful everyone might be, accidents do happen and a dog can manage to escape from the crate. Include on the tag a telephone number at which someone can be reached 24 hours a day. When you reach your destination, do not remove your dog from the crate unless you are in a safe enclosed area. There are cases of owners opening the crate at

arrival and their dog bolting out in panic without even realizing the owner was there.

8. Arrive early. Get to the airport a minimum of two hours before flight time. Go directly to the passenger check-in counter. Make sure your Bichon is fully checked in but insist that you stay where you can see the dog until it is time to send the crate to the loading area. At that point make a headlong dash for the gate and try and find a window where you can see baggage being loaded on to your plane. When you get on board have the flight attendant check to make sure the dog actually is on board. Most are glad to do so once they get all their passengers on and seated. This may make you feel like a bit of a nuisance, but that age-old saw, "the squeaking wheel gets the grease," certainly applies here.

If Your Bichon Can't Come with You

Not all destinations are appropriate for your Bichon. What then, short of canceling your trip? There are viable alternatives.

I'm aware that no one can take care of little Pierre as you do, but there just may be a person or boarding kennel out there that can do it well. In fact they might do such a bang-up job your dog will love it!

Doggie Dude Ranches

The only way you can find that person or place, however, is by doing a lot of checking. To help steer you in the right direction your veterinarian may be able to offer recommendations of local facilities known to have earned high marks for pet care. There is also an organization called the American Boarding Kennel Association that can do likewise. Your breeder may also have recommendations, and so may your neighbors.

No kennel is adequate for your Bichon unless the place meets *your* approval. Drop by during one or two business hours and ask for a tour. Understand that few kennels are

going to be as neat and spiffy as your kitchen or living room. Imagine your own home with a couple of dozen dogs in it. It's hard to keep any kennel smelling like your home, but bad smells and smells that hang through the air no matter where you go don't offer the promise of sanitary conditions.

Check to see if food and water containers are kept clean. Do the runs show signs of regular care and cleaning? Look at what the surface of the runs is made of. Do the surfaces provide good footing and easy cleanup and sanitizing? What provisions are made for exercise? What about security—are the runs escape proof?

Even though your practically perfect Pierre would never provoke a fight, a dog housed next to him at a kennel might encourage Pierre to do battle. Look at the fencing and make sure it provides safety without making the dog feel cut off from the world. Metal mesh between runs ensures that beards and fluffy tails stay attached to the proper owner but the dogs are still able to see each other.

Ask the kennel manager and employees what their views of Bichons are. The best-behaved Bichon at home can become a delinquent when a part of a kennel gang.

If your Bichon wants and needs attention, make sure the kennel attendants will provide this. Many kennels provide what they call "play time"—an interval in a large paddock and someone to play catch with. The cost may be a few dollars more per day for this service, but it can mean a big difference in your pal's stay.

Find out what inoculations and health precautions boarders are required to have at check in. Most demand proof of current rabies inoculations and protection against kennel cough. It's important to know if incoming dogs are screened for fleas, ticks, and other parasites. If there are no health safeguards requirements, your Bichon won't come home as healthy as when he left.

Always leave your veterinarian's name, address, and phone number in case of emergency. Also leave contact numbers where you can be reached at all times while you're gone. Provide Pierre's blanket and plenty of his favorite toys. Check on the food the kennel feeds before you arrive, and if you do not feel that it is suitable for your dog you must bring enough of your Bichon's accustomed food to last for the duration of your absence.

Pet Sitters

You may feel there is no way that you would consider sentencing your pal to time in one of those boarding "prisons." If that's the case, think about a pet sitter. A pet sitter is someone who will come to your home at regular intervals during the day to feed, provide time for your dog to exercise, and take care of those calls of nature. If your Bichon isn't happier with this arrangement

than in a boarding kennel, at least you will be.

Maybe you have a friend or relative that gets along well with your Bichon who will be happy to do this for a day, or perhaps even two days. But if your absence will extend beyond that, do consider paying someone to take care of what must be done. No matter how charming your friends find your Bichon when they visit, having to interrupt their lives to attend to someone else's dog day after day can be a burden. Here again, your veterinarian may be able to recommend someone, and there are national organizations dedicated to making recommendations for qualified pet sitters. See Useful Addresses and Literature later in this book.

It is best to hire a professional pet sitter for many reasons. Most professionals provide credentials and written agreements to what they will be responsible for. In your case, you want a sitter who knows and understands the Bichon and with whom your Bichon will be compatible.

Professional pet sitters who are members of a national pet-sitting organization are usually bonded and insured. This is very important in that any dog lover can advertise as a "professional," but loving dogs is not insurance against dishonesty. You don't want to return to find your Bichon in a house stripped of your valuables.

Entrusting your Bichon and your entire household to a perfect stranger is a serious step. There are a number of "bottom line" requirements.

A professional pet sitter is often the best answer to providing for your dog when you cannot be there to do it yourself.

Speak to an official of the organization the prospective sitter belongs to and ask for written certification that the sitter is bonded and insured. Ask if the organization has clients' evaluation of the sitter.

Find out what experience the prospective sitter has had with small dogs and Bichons specifically. A good sitter doesn't need to have worked with Bichons, but should have a good sense of how smaller dogs should be dealt with.

Read the sitter's agreement carefully to see if it covers everything that is important to *you*. What is omitted should be added in writing. The agreement should include all information the sitter needs to know about your dog, your home, and related responsibilities.

Find out if the sitter has a 24-hour pager or cell phone to be reached quickly at any hour. You should also know if there is an alternate for the sitter in case of the sitter's illness or accident. Make a record of the phone numbers of both those individuals. Obviously the sitter should also be provided with your 24-hour contact information.

Both you and the sitter have to discuss and agree on the charges for services rendered. If you have given the sitter an accurate list of what you expect, there will be no confusion as to what will be charged for and what will be performed gratis.

Chapter Twelve

Genetic Diseases and Parasites

The well-bred and well-raised Bichon Frise is basically a very healthy dog with a love of humans and extroverted personality that is the envy of owners of many other breeds. The breed is long-lived, and properly cared for will give you and your family years of companionship and pleasure. With all-important preventive maintenance you won't have to worry about renting space at your veterinarian's office. However, having to care for a chronically ill Bichon is not only an unhappy situation, it costs a good amount of money.

Genetic Diseases

Like all breeds of domesticated dogs, including the mixed breeds, the Bichon has its share of hereditary problems. What is described here will be far less apt to be present in the Bichon you buy from reputable breeders—particularly those who are members of the BFCA—because in a majority of cases their stock is test bred and rigidly selected to avoid these problems as much as possible. Even though these breeders constantly test and do their utmost to breed around inheritable problems, they are not God. Any one of those problems can arise in even the best-planned litter.

The problems that exist in the breed should be discussed with the breeder from whom you purchase your dog. If you ever suspect symptoms of the problems occurring, you should speak to your breeder first or at the very least make an appointment to see your veterinarian without delay.

Genetic testing and screening are an important part of all current breeding programs by those who have genuine concern for the health and welfare of their dogs. All the care that preceded the birth of your puppy is what has made this Bichon a healthy individual. That health must be safeguarded through consistent care and diligence.

Please refer to the notice (pages 118–121) from the BFCA regarding the work the club does to rid the breed of genetic problems that can exist within the breed. Additional information on these concerns can be found on the BFCA Web site or by contacting the BFCA directly.

Vaccinations

Every Bichon puppy that comes from a respected kennel has at least begun an immunization protocol against the major canine diseases. These diseases are distemper, leptospirosis, hepatitis, and canine parvovirus. Your puppy may also have received a temporary vaccination against distemper, but ask the breeder to be sure.

The age at which vaccinations are given can vary, but will usually be when the puppy is 8 to 12 weeks old. By this time any protection given to the Bichon puppy by antibodies from its mother's milk will be losing its strength.

A puppy's immune system works because white blood cells destroy attacking bacteria. However, the white cells must first recognize a potential enemy. Vaccines are made up of either dead or live bacteria. If they are alive the bacteria exist in very small doses. Either type prompts the puppy's defense system to attack them. The immune system recognizes a large bacterial attack and massive numbers of lymphocytes (white blood corpuscles) are mobilized to counter the attack.

However, the ability of the cells to recognize these dangerous viruses can decrease over time. Therefore it is important to provide the immune system with the annual "reminders" of booster injections. Although immunization is not an iron-clad guarantee of immunity against a particular disease, it is the most successful strategy thus far. Certainly it is better than giving a puppy no protection at all.

On rare occasions immunization does not confer full immunity against infectious diseases. Therefore it is important to detect signs of these illnesses in case your Bichon is one of the few who are not immune and actually do develop the diseases.

Canine Parvovirus

This is a particularly infectious gastrointestinal disease commonly referred to as "parvo" and can be contracted by direct contact or by being exposed to areas in which infected dogs have been housed. While dogs of all ages can be and are infected by canine parvovirus, this disease is particularly fatal to puppies. Symptoms include acute diarrhea, often bloody with yellow or gray stools. Soaring body temperatures, sometimes as high as 106 degrees, are not uncommon, particularly in puppies. Death can follow as quickly as one to three days after first symptoms appear. Early treatment is critical. If there is any suspicion of this disease, contact your veterinarian at once!

Canine Distemper

Extremely high fever can be the first sign of this very serious and often fatal disease. Mortality among puppies and adults that have not

The Bichon Frise is basically a very healthy dog with a love of humans and an extroverted personality that is the envy of owners of many other breeds. This is particularly true of the dogs that come from the lines established by many of our longtime breeders.

been immunized is extremely high. Other signs may be loss of appetite, diarrhea, and blood in the stools, followed by dehydration. Respiratory infections of all kinds are apt to accompany these conditions. Symptoms can appear as quickly as a week after exposure.

Hardpad

This is considered to be a secondary infection. Hardpad often accompanies distemper. A symptom is hardening of the pads of the dog's feet, but the virus eventually attacks the central nervous system, causing convulsions and encephalitis.

Infectious Hepatitis

Infectious canine hepatitis is a liver infection of particularly extreme virulence. It is a different virus from that which affects people, but it affects some of the same organs. It eventually affects many other parts of the body with varying degrees of intensity, so that the infected dog can run the range of reactions from watery eyes, listlessness, and loss of appetite to violent trembling, labored breathing, vomiting, and extreme thirst. Infection normally occurs through exposure to the urine of animals affected with the disease. Symptoms can appear within a week of exposure.

Leptospirosis

Leptospirosis is a bacterial disease contracted by direct exposure to the urine of an animal affected with the disease. *Both wild and domestic animals are affected by leptospirosis, and an animal can contract it from simply sniffing a tree or bush on which an affected animal has urinated.*

Leptospirosis is not prevalent in all sections of the country, so the problem should be discussed with your veterinarian, particularly if you intend to travel with your dog. "Lepto" can be contagious to humans as well as animals and can be fatal to both.

Rapidly fluctuating temperatures, total loss of maneuverability, bleeding gums, and bloody diarrhea are all signs. Mortality rate is extremely high.

Rabies

Rabies infection normally occurs through a bite from an infected animal. The likelihood of your Bichon's coming in contact with a rabid dog is very remote, but remember that all mammals are subject to infection. Your Bichon may want to play with a squirrel or some other wild creature out of doors and be bitten while attempting to do so.

The rabies virus affects the central nervous system through inflammation of the spinal cord and central nervous system. Rabies symptoms may not be as quick to appear or as detectable as in other diseases because they often resemble the symptoms of other less virulent diseases. Withdrawal and personality change are common symptoms, as well as the many symptoms accompanying the other infectious diseases already described.

Optional or "the law"? There are no ordinances regarding vaccinating your dog against any of the communicable diseases other than rabies. The rabies vaccine is not without risk in isolated cases, but the possibility of a negative reaction is far outweighed by the consequences of contracting the disease. It is extremely important that you keep your dog's rabies inoculations current and that the tag issued by your

Any person bitten by any animal, wild or domestic, that is suspected of being rabid should call their personal physician at once! If a suspected animal bites your dog, call your veterinarian without delay.

veterinarian is attached to your dog's collar. If your dog should ever bite someone, you must be able to offer proof of current rabies inoculation. If not, your dog may, by law, be held in quarantine for a considerable length of time to determine the possibility of rabies infection. *Rabies inoculations are not optional!*

Kennel Cough

Kennel cough, or bordatella, while highly infectious, is actually not a serious disease. It might be compared to a mild case of the flu in human beings. Infected dogs act and eat normally. The symptoms of the disease are far worse than the disease itself. Particularly nerve-wracking is the persistent hacking cough that sounds as if the dog will bring up everything it has eaten.

The name of the disease is misleading in that it indicates a dog must be exposed to a kennel environment to be infected. In reality it can be easily passed from one dog to another with even casual contact.

In severe cases of kennel cough antibiotics are sometimes prescribed to avoid secondary infec-

Bichon Health

From the Bichon Frise Club of America

All too often, buying a puppy is an impulse purchase. Once the puppy gets home, the new owner decides to learn more about the breed and investigates potential size, temperament, and how to feed this cuddly creature. Rarely does he or she check out potential health problems. Yet many of the contacts made to the Bichon Frise Club of America's internet site at *www.bichon.org* are from pet owners needing advice or reporting health problems on our web health survey site.

There are several principals in buying a pet that need to be addressed, and the first is that the best way to find a healthy puppy is to buy one with healthy parents, grandparents, and great-grandparents.

It is important to know that at least four generations of the ancestors have not exhibited symptoms of genetic disease. The reason for this is that even those dogs free of a given disease may still carry genes for the disease. If both parents have the gene for that disease, some of the pups may then be affected. Those dogs free of disease symptoms but having the genes are called *carriers*.

And Bichons do have certain inherited diseases. The most common health problem in Bichons is *allergy*. Inhalant allergy *(atopy)* may be mild and seasonal and may or may not need treatment. Spring and fall are usually the worst times.

For the Bichon with flea allergy, even a single fleabite can cause extreme itching and misery. Food allergies are relatively rare but can be the cause of intestinal problems as well as skin irritation. For the allergic Bichon being treated for itchy skin, the continued use of steroids such as prednisone can set him up for another illness later in life (more about that illness later). It is much safer to use the milder antihistamines to control scratching, and those only as needed. *Note: Probably half of all Bichons need treatment for allergy at some time in their lives. Some Bichons have severe allergies and require extensive testing and treatment to relieve the symptoms. Allergy cannot be cured.*

Inherited cataracts can eventually cause blindness. Cataracts occur in many breeds and usually begin to form in the Bichon by age seven. However some very young dogs become blind (before their first birthday). It is very important to know that at least several generations of ancestors have been registered with the Canine Eye Registration Foundation (known as CERF) as clear of cataracts. To determine if the dog has early cataracts requires a special examination by a veterinary ophthalmologist and your personal veterinarian will most likely not be able to diagnose them until they are fully formed. Although fewer than 10 percent of Bichons have blinding cataracts, another 30 to 40 percent may be carriers. BFCA sponsored research that has determined that cataracts in Bichons are a recessive trait and research continues to find a DNA marker so that breeding stock can be tested for the gene prior to breeding. Surgery may or may not correct the problem, and some Bichons suffer retinal detachment during surgery. Therefore it may be advisable to operate on only one eye at a time.

Bladder stones (*urolithiasis)* and bladder infections are considered one of the primary health issues in the breed. *Struvite* stones are caused by infection and this type is not considered to be inherited, though there may be a breed predisposition to infection. Possibly *gingivitis*, or gum disease, contributes to the problem, meaning it is vital to practice good dental hygiene in Bichons. Infections in the mouth can cause germs to be spread to other organs or the bladder via the bloodstream. *Calcium oxalate* stones, are inherited and the calcium stones, if not properly treated, may eventually have a coating of struvite, causing a missed diagnosis. Only the correct type of analysis will determine the type of stone at the core. For more information on Bichon bladder stones, see *www.bichon.org/stones.htm*.

There are also inherited orthopedic problems, the most common being *luxating patellas*, or loose kneecaps. Ruptured spinal disc, found more often in Bichons that are longer in body, overweight, and with short legs, is diagnosed in a small number of Bichons. *Hip dysplasia* and a hip problem called *Legg-Calve-Perthes* are occasionally diagnosed in the breed. For each of these orthopedic problems, surgery may eventually be needed but avoiding obesity in the pet may help to avoid surgery. To determine if the parents have been screened for orthopedic problems, look for the OFA number on your Bichon's AKC registration certificate. This indicates registration with the Orthopedic Foundation for Animals. (OFA registry includes several screening procedures, so it is necessary to determine which condition was registered and you can do so at *http://www.offa.org*.)

And we come to the second principal in finding a healthy pet: check **the parents pedigree and registration papers to see if there are also Canine Eye Registration Foundation (CERF) and Orthopedic Foundation for Animals (OFA) registration numbers, proving the parents have been screened for**

inherited eye and orthopedic disease. The AKC number only proves that the parents have been registered as purebred and is not a guarantee of health.

Other diseases occurring with less frequency are *diabetes*, *Cushings syndrome,* and *pancreatitis*, each of which has a possible inherited component making the dog more susceptible to these conditions. Diabetes often comes along with obesity, so keeping the dog slim (not skinny) may help avoid that one. Cushings syndrome may be inherited, but it may also be precipitated by overuse of steroids, often used to treat allergies. It is best to use prednisone only in severe situations and for a limited time and always according to veterinary instructions. Whenever possible, try antihistamine treatment first and consider testing the severely allergic dog to find the offending pollen, mold, or other allergens. As to pancreatitis, this is usually an illness requiring fast treatment to avoid permanent harm to the dog, so discuss this illness with your veterinarian so you are familiar with the signs.

Heart disease, liver disease, and other common health issues can occur in any breed and are found in some Bichons. It is important for the dog that you have him examined at least once or twice a year as a matter of routine. He should have his teeth cleaned twice a year by the veterinary clinician, with daily brushing at home. Any dramatic change in behavior should alert the owner to schedule a visit to the clinic for an examination. The earlier treated, the faster any of these problems will be resolved.

Immunization schedules are changing and the pet may not need annual boosters unless required by local law (as with rabies), and titers can be checked after the first combination booster to determine the need for future boosters. **If the dog needs both the rabies shot and the combination shot, BFCA strongly recommends that these shots be separated by at least a month in order not to stress the immune system of your Bichon.**

With so many diseases being mentioned as occurring in Bichons, it would seem that this breed has many health problems. This is not actually the case. The breed has until now been relatively healthy, and responsible breeders are making every effort to keep them vital and well. Unfortunately the breed has also become extremely popular and unwise breeding occurs. Sometimes we hear from owners of a Bichon that has had every one of the above-mentioned problems, all in the same dog! We know then that the so-called breeder of this unfortunate dog had no knowledge of the genetic background of the parents—or was more interested in making money off a popular breed than in producing healthy puppies.

This leads us to the last principal of buying a healthy dog. This may be the most important one of all. **Spay or neuter you puppy as soon as it has reached the age recommended by your veterinarian!** You found a breed that you care about and you can do your part to maintain good health by NOT breeding your beloved pet. Without full knowledge of several generations of ancestors, you cannot possibly know if a Bichon is affected by or a carrier of faulty genes. As an added bonus, the chances of a female developing mammary cancer is totally eliminated when spayed early and the male will be unlikely to have prostate cancer, two of the most common fatal illnesses in dogs!

BFCA is doing its part in maintaining health in this beautiful breed of dogs. To date over $50,000 has been invested in health research into cataracts and allergies, and more research is planned in these and other diseases. Our members sell their puppies with a contract requiring buyers to spay or neuter pets, and most can substantiate many generations of breeding stock that have been screened for genetic disease. It is important to the future of the breed to eliminate affected dogs and carriers from the gene pool. It is the intent of the Bichon Frise Club of America to make every effort to do so with restricted breeding and research. The dog owner can play a vital part by following the lead of responsible breeders and neutering their pets. Contributions to canine health research may be a way to honor your pets and to aid in improving the breed.

To learn more about the Bichon Frise, its care and training, health information, rescue efforts, and other important facts, visit the official BFCA web site at www.bichon.org.

Anne Jones
BFCA Health and
Education Committee

Contributions to the health research fund can be made to the Bichon Frise Club of America via the club treasurer or to the American Kennel Club Canine Health Foundation designated for the Bichon Frise Donor Advised Fund. More information is available at www.bichon.org.

tions such as pneumonia, but various protective procedures can be administered by your veterinarian. An intranasal vaccine is available to provide immunity.

These protective measures are advised for your Bichon, particularly if your dog visits a dog park or is taken to a boarding kennel. In fact, most boarding kennels now insist upon proof of protection against kennel cough before they will accept a dog for boarding.

Many Bichon breeders are opposed to the 5, 6, and 7 in 1 modified live vaccines (DHLPP). Some Bichon puppies get very ill within two or three days of receiving the vaccines, or within a couple of weeks later. In other cases seizures and/or symptoms of hypothyroidism, liver and kidney problems, and heart complications show up to a greater or lesser degree several years later. A good many breeders recommend giving separate shots over a gradual period. Discuss this with the breeder from whom you purchase your Bichon puppy and insist your veterinarian follow those recommendations to the letter.

Parasites—Inside and Out

Your Bichon is susceptible to parasitic invasions internally and externally. There is even one form of parasite that is both internal and external. Regular grooming, cleanliness, and biannual stool examinations by your veterinarian can keep down the infestations but do not be surprised that even with your best efforts some of these nasty creatures will find their way into your home or inside your Bichon.

External Parasites

Fleas. No matter how careful you might be in the care of your Bichon, fleas can still be a problem. By just playing in the yard or even on daily walks your dog can bring fleas into your home, and once there these nasty little creatures multiply with amazing speed. Cats with outdoor access compound this already difficult problem by attracting fleas on their neighborhood patrols and bringing them back home on their fur.

Bichons who live in northern climates where there are heavy frosts and freezing temperatures have winter relief from the flea. Fleas can't survive these conditions. Bichons who live in the warmer climates face the flea problem all year round.

A word to the wise—flea baths will not solve the problem. If you find even one flea on your dog, there probably are hundreds, maybe thousands of them, lurking in the carpeting and furniture throughout your home. The minute after a dog's bath, the fleas are ready, willing, and able to hop back on.

Aside from the discomfort, Bichons are extremely sensitive to flea bites, and severe scratching begins. This can quickly lead to "hot spots." A dog's chewing and scratching so hard that the skin is broken creates hot spots. If not treated promptly, these sores can form moist, painful abscesses and all hair surrounding the area falls off.

Life cycle of the flea. Fleas also act as carriers of tapeworm eggs. When a dog swallows a flea, the tapeworm eggs grow in the dog's intestines. If your Ami has fleas you

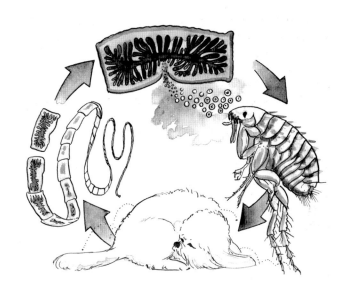

Life cycle of the tapeworm: Fleas are commonly hosts of the tapeworm. When the flea is swallowed, the parasite is shared with your dog, tapeworms develop, and segments are passed in the feces.

can bet your bottom dollar that she'll have tapeworms as well. Tapeworms will be dealt with further under "Internal Parasites."

Once Ami has been infested with fleas there is only one sure-fire way of eliminating the problem and keeping it in check. It takes planning but is well worth the time

Make an appointment for your Bichon to be given a flea bath by your veterinarian or local grooming parlor. Most groomers use products that will completely rid your Bichon of existing fleas.

While your dog is away being bathed, have a commercial pest control service come to your home. If you or Ami return home before this is done, the fleas will be back within hours (minutes?). The service will spray both the interior of your home and the surrounding property. Most

of these companies guarantee the effectiveness of their work for several months.

While the extermination process is going on, your home must be vacated and kept closed for at least a few hours following the spraying.

Flea control products. The day your Bichon comes home from the groomer, apply a flea control product that can be used on an ongoing basis. These products control fleas by stopping their life cycle. The nice thing about these products is that they have no deadly effect on mammals at all.

There are pills you can give your dog or liquids that are placed on the dog's skin between the shoulder blades. Following directions regularly, these preventives are highly effective in keeping both fleas and ticks off household pets.

Tick Removal

To remove a tick from your Bichon, carefully part the hair so that the individual tick is clearly visible. Soak it with a tick removal solution that can be purchased at most complete pet shops. When the tick releases its grip, you can remove it with a pair of tweezers. The tick must loosen its grip before you attempt to remove it. If the tick hasn't let go, the little beast's head can be separated from its body. If the tick's head is allowed to remain lodged in your Bichon's skin, it could cause a severe infection. After the tick is removed, swab the area with alcohol to avoid infection.

Always use latex gloves and tweezers to avoid the possibility of infecting yourself if the tick is a disease carrier. Wash your hands and any instruments you've used with alcohol. If you suspect your area to be infested with disease-carrying ticks, put the tick in a bottle or baggie and take it to your veterinarian without delay for testing.

Do not flush the tick in the toilet. They can survive the swim! Never crush the tick between your fingers because that will expose you to any disease the tick might be carrying. The best way to eliminate a tick permanently is to put it into a jar with a bit of alcohol and screw the lid on tightly.

Some of the same insect growth regulators that control fleas also do an excellent job of keeping ticks off your dog. Ask your veterinarian to recommend effective products.

Lice. Well-cared-for Bichons seldom encounter a problem with lice since these parasites are spread by direct contact. Your Bichon will have to spend time with another animal that has lice or be groomed with a contaminated brush or comb in order to be at risk.

If no fleas are present and you do suspect lice, your Bichon will have to be bathed with an insecticide shampoo every week until the problem is eradicated. Lice live and breed exclusively on the dog itself, so it will not be necessary to follow the procedure required to rid your dog of fleas.

Ticks. If you live near a wooded area you are bound to run across at least the occasional tick. Your Bichon can pick up these parasites just running through grass or brush. Ticks are bloodsucking parasites that bury their heads firmly into a dog's skin. The ticks gorge themselves on the dog's blood and then find a dark little corner to raise little ticks, and their number can swell to hundreds before you know it!

Ticks represent a serious health hazard to both humans and other animals. In some areas ticks carry Lyme disease and Rocky Mountain spotted fever. The entire area in

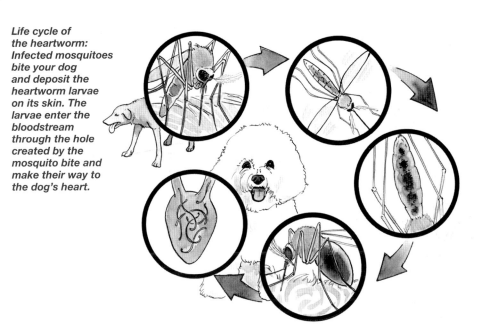

Life cycle of the heartworm: Infected mosquitoes bite your dog and deposit the heartworm larvae on its skin. The larvae enter the bloodstream through the hole created by the mosquito bite and make their way to the dog's heart.

which the dog lives must be aggressively treated against ticks with sprays and dips made especially for that purpose.

Mange. There are two kinds of mange—demodectic and sarcoptic. Both are caused by mites and must be treated by your veterinarian.

Demodectic mange (*Demodex canis*) is believed to be present on practically all dogs without creating undue harm to the affected dog. Only about one percent of all dogs ever develop clinical symptoms.

There are two different forms of demodectic mange: local and general. Bichons affected locally may lose the hair around their eyes and in small patches on the chest and forelegs. This form can be easily treated by a veterinarian and must

not be neglected, because occasionally the local form can develop into the more severe, generalized form.

Sarcoptic mange (*Sarcoptes scabiei* var *canis*) is also known as scabies and can be present over the entire dog. Symptoms include loss of hair on legs and ears, often in patches over the entire body. Your veterinarian must do a skin scraping to identify the type and prescribe treatment. Weekly bathing with medications especially formulated for this parasite can usually eliminate the problem. This type of mange is passed on by direct contact and is highly contagious.

Internal Parasites

The most common internal parasites are roundworms, tapeworms, and heartworms. All three are best diagnosed and treated by your veterinarian. Great advances are continually being made in dealing with these parasites; what used to be complicated, messy, and time-consuming treatments have been replaced and simplified over the years.

Tapeworms. Tapeworms are a part of the life cycle of the flea. If your Bichon has or had fleas you will undoubtedly have to deal with tapeworms. Tapeworms are small rice-like segments of the worm that may be found crawling around your Bichon's anus or in the stool just after the dog has relieved itself.

Periodic stool examinations done by your veterinarian can determine the presence of tapeworms, even though you may not observe the segments yourself. There is an inoculation your veterinarian can administer that quickly and completely eliminates the problem.

Heartworms. Heartworms are parasitic worms found in dogs' hearts. The worm is transmitted by mosquitoes that carry the larvae of the worm. Dogs are the only mammals that are commonly affected and the condition is far more prevalent in warmer climates that have longer periods of time for mosquitoes to reproduce. Blood tests can detect the presence of this worm and a veterinarian can prescribe oral medication for both preventive and corrective measures.

Whipworms and Hookworms. These two worms are shed in a dog's stool and can live for long periods in the soil. Both worms can attach themselves to the skin of humans as well as animals and eventually burrow their way to the lining of the intestines. They are then seldom passed or seen. These two worms are detected only by microscopic examination of the stool, and each worm requires specific medication to ensure elimination.

Roundworms. Roundworms are not unusual and are seldom harmful to adult dogs. However, these parasites can be hazardous to the health of Bichon puppies if allowed to progress unchecked. Roundworms are transmitted from mother to puppies. Responsible breeders make sure their females are free of worms before they are bred. Roundworms can sometimes be visible in a dog's stool but are best detected by your veterinarian in a microscopic examination of a fresh stool sample. Puppies affected by roundworms have dull and dry-looking coats and the puppies themselves appear thin but at the same time have "pot bellies."

Your puppy should receive regular physical examinations or checkups. One form is obviously performed by your veterinarian, and the other is a daily procedure that should be done by you. Apart from the fact that the exam will reveal any problem at an early stage, it is an excellent way of socializing the pup to being handled.

Chapter Thirteen
Safety First

Accidents happen. It's a simple fact of life. As careful as you might be with your Bichon, there is no way to protect it from every hazard. Your veterinarian and 24-hour emergency clinics are there to help when the need arises, but there are times when immediate care is critical. If you aren't prepared it could mean your dog's life.

Discuss emergencies with your veterinarian, who may have products or devices that you may not have thought of or don't even know exist. What follows are some emergency procedures and the basics for a first aid kit. This information is not meant to substitute for the knowledge and experience your own veterinarian has spent a lifetime accumulating. There will be times though that your know-how could prevent relatively minor situations developing into serious complications.

When to Call Your Veterinarian

If you are in doubt how to handle any health problem, telephone your veterinarian who will know the questions to ask to determine whether it is necessary to bring your Bichon into the hospital or if there is an emergency procedure you should begin at once.

There's hardly a dog that doesn't at one time or another get into something that will cause vomiting or diarrhea. If this occurs it does not necessarily mean your dog is seriously ill, but if it should continue, don't hesitate to call your veterinarian. Bichons will often purge their digestive tracts by eating grass to induce vomiting. Puppies will often vomit when they have eaten too much or too fast. Mothers with young litters will often eat and then regurgitate their food in order to begin to wean their puppies.

Switching your dog's regular diet to a bland diet best treats occasional diarrhea. Thoroughly cooked rice with a very small amount of boiled chicken or chicken broth is always tempting and eases the digestive tract. Keep your Bichon on this diet until the diarrhea is controlled and then very gradually add your dog's regular food over a period of several days.

What to Do When You Need to Do It

Muzzling

There are basic lifesaving techniques every dog owner should know. Always exercise extreme care in dealing with very ill or injured animals. Don't forget where you and I use our hands in automatic response to pain, a dog will use its mouth. Although Pierre would never think of biting you or anyone else, any dog in extreme pain may snap or bite.

If this occurs, your having to deal with your own emergency will not help your dog. Always muzzle your dog before beginning any first aid technique that may cause even what you might consider mild pain!

A nylon stocking is strong and will not cut or irritate the dog's muzzle. Snugly wrap the center section of the stocking twice around your Bichon's muzzle. Do not wrap too tightly so that it is uncomfortable, but do so firmly enough to keep your dog from using his jaws to bite. Tie the two remaining ends of the stocking under the jaw, draw them back behind the dog's ears, and tie them there.

First Aid Techniques for You to Master

Moving an injured Bichon. Moving an injured Bichon is relatively easy for the person of even average strength. However, you want as much as possible to avoid jostling your dog. Lay him on a large bath towel or blanket and fold the material around him with only his head emerging. This will help immobilize him. Do your best to move the dog into your car with as little disturbance as possible. If you have someone to accompany you, place your dog on the back seat and have the person with you keep a steadying and reassuring hand on the dog until you reach your veterinarian. If you are alone it is best to place your dog, blanket and all, inside a shipping crate.

Burns. Applying cold water or a cold compress can treat minor burns. Gauze pads can be used to apply an antibiotic cream. Cover the

Muzzling: A discarded nylon stocking will work well to secure your Bichon's jaws while administering first aid. To apply an emergency muzzle, follow the instructions in the text.

Your Bichon's First Aid Kit

A metal box with a lid that can be securely closed is the ideal container for your first-aid supplies. Many homes have a box of this type that contains the family's emergency supplies. Purchase another for your Bichon, but mark it carefully on the lid with your Bichon's name. You can also purchase ready-made canine emergency kits at veterinary hospitals and pet emporiums. Clearly print on the lid the name, address, and telephone number of your regular veterinarian. Also include the address and phone number of the nearest 24-hour emergency veterinary hospital and the telephone number of the National Animal Poison Control Center. The phone number for the Center can be found in Useful Addresses and Literature.

Check the kit regularly to replace used or evaporated materials.

- Rectal thermometer
- Eyewash
- Antibiotic ointment (eyes) and powder (skin)
- Nylon stocking (to use as muzzle)
- Adhesive bandaging tape
- Tweezers
- Antibacterial ointment (for skin and eyes)
- Scissors (preferably with rounded tips)
- Gauze rolls and dressing pads
- Tourniquet kit
- Blanket or heavy toweling
- Cotton balls
- Diarrhea medicine
- Activated charcoal tablets
- Antihistamine (veterinarian-approved for allergic reactions)
- Hydrogen peroxide (3 percent solution)
- Ipecac syrup (to induce vomiting)
- K-Y Jelly
- Rubbing alcohol
- Syringe (without needle, for administering oral medications)
- Rubber gloves

Every dog owner should have a fully supplied First Aid Kit on hand at all times. A metal box with a lid that can be securely closed is the ideal container.

Moving an injured Bichon: Avoid jostling the dog as much as possible. Lay him on a large bath towel or blanket, and then fold the material around him with only his head emerging.

burn with a gauze pad that can be held in place with an elastic bandage. Serious burns or scalding need your veterinarian's attention at once. Cool down burned area with very cool water or cover with water-soaked washcloths.

Shock. Your Bichon may go into shock as a result of electrocution, burn, or injury. If the dog is unconscious, check to be sure that the airway is open. Clear fluids and secretions from the mouth with your fingers or a washcloth. Pull the tip of the tongue foreword beyond the front teeth to make breathing easier. Keep the head lower than the body by placing a blanket or pillow beneath the hindquarters. Cover him with another blanket to keep the dog warm on the way to the veterinarian's office.

If your Bichon is not breathing, begin artificial respiration at once! To give a Bichon artificial respiration place the dog on his side on a table with his head lower than his body. Close your dog's mouth by wrapping your hand around the muzzle, insuring that you do not cause his teeth to close over his tongue.

Next place your mouth over the dog's nose, and blow into his nostrils. The chest should expand. Release your mouth to let the dog exhale. Repeat so your dog gets 20 breaths per minute, one breath every three seconds. Continue the procedure until your dog is breathing on his own.

Bites and bleeding wounds. If your Bichon is bleeding, you must attend to the wounds at once. If the flow of blood is not stemmed, your dog could bleed to death. Apply pressure directly to the bleeding point with a cotton pad or compress soaked in cold water. If bleeding continues, you must seek your veterinarian's advice.

Should your Bichon be bitten by another dog or animal get your dog to the veterinarian without delay. Even the most minor bite wounds can be infected and should get antibiotic treatment immediately.

Poisons. Always keep current and available the telephone numbers of your local or national poison control center and the local 24-hour emergency veterinary hospital. If you know or suspect what kind of poison your dog has ingested, give this information to the poison control center; they may be able to prescribe an immediate antidote. Inform your veterinarian of any information the poison control center gives you.

Household products can be extremely dangerous if your dog eats or drinks them. Antifreeze, paint thinners, chocolate, and many decorative plants could easily take your dog's life. Read labels and discuss potentially harmful household items with your veterinarian.

If you are not sure if your Bichon has been poisoned or if you do not know which poison the dog may have ingested, be prepared to describe the symptoms to the poison control center or your veterinarian. Common symptoms of poisoning are: paralysis, convulsions, tremors, diarrhea, vomiting, and stomach cramps accompanied by howling, heavy breathing, and whimpering.

Broken bones. Although the Bichon's bone structure is such that the bones are not easily broken, that doesn't mean it can never happen. If you suspect your Bichon has broken a bone, remain calm. If the injury is not handled correctly and immediately, serious complications can arise. Panic on your part can upset your dog further and cause him to thrash around, making matters even worse.

If your Bichon is unable to stand or if one of his legs is held at an unnatural angle, or if the dog reacts painfully to being touched, support your dog's body as much as possible. If a blanket or coat is available, slip this under the dog and move him as gently as you are able.

Don't try and guess at how serious the injuries may be. You are not able to determine the extent of internal bleeding and damage. Get your Bichon to the veterinarian's office at

Some Harmful House Plants
- Airplane plant
- Azalea
- Caladium
- Cyclamen
- Diffenbachia
- Foxglove
- Holly
- Jerusalem cherry
- Mistletoe
- Mother-in-law's tongue
- Philodendron
- Poinsettia
- Rhododendron
- Spider plant
- Yew

once. If there is someone available to drive you and your dog to the veterinary hospital, all the better. That way you will be able to devote your attention to keeping your dog calm and immobile.

Foreign Objects and Choking

Lodged objects: Puppies are born vacuum cleaners and even adult Bichons delight in taking into their mouths objects on the floor or out in the yard. It isn't unusual for these objects to get lodged or trapped across their teeth, usually halfway back, or even where the two jaws hinge. If you see your Bichon pawing at his mouth or rubbing his jaws along the ground, check to see if there is something lodged in his mouth.

If something is lodged in the dog's jaws, grasp the object firmly between your fingers and push firmly toward the back of the mouth where the teeth are wider apart. This normally dislodges the object, but be sure to have a firm grip on the object so the dog does not swallow it. If the object does not come loose immediately get your Bichon to your veterinarian.

Swallowed objects. If the object is not visible in your dog's mouth it may have already been swallowed. If it is still present in the dog's throat he may be choking. Wedge something like a closed ballpoint pen or similar object in the dog's mouth to keep the jaws open.

Pulling the tongue out should reveal any objects lodged at the back of the throat. If so, grasp the object firmly and pull it out. If the dog seems to be having trouble breathing, the object could be lodged in the windpipe. Sharp firm pressure to the rib cage can help make the dog expel air from the lungs and expel the object as well. Moderate the intensity of your blows to the rib cage to avoid damage to the ribs.

Heatstroke

The easiest way for a Bichon to get heatstroke is for the dog to be left in a car in hot weather. The temperature of a dog in heatstroke soars above the normal 100 to 102.5 degrees and breath is very rapid but shallow. It is critical to cool the dog down at once either in a tub of cool water or with a garden hose. Place ice packs on the abdomen, head, neck, and body. Cover the body with water-cooled towels. Call your veterinarian at once.

Hypothermia

In northern climates a Bichon may also be in danger of hypothermia, in which the dog's body temperature drops below normal—even a few degrees could spell danger. A dog's heart rate increases significantly and shivering sets in when a dog is in hypothermia. Immersion in warm water or wrapping the dog in warmed blankets or heating pads will bring the dog's temperature back to normal. If the dog's mouth and tongue begin to turn blue this is a sign that circulation is closing down. Warm the dog as much as possible and call your veterinarian!

Things you never considered dangerous can be lethal to the inquisitive and mischievous Bichon puppy. Think of your puppy as one part private investigator and one part vacuum cleaner, and you'll have some idea of what to expect.

The Bichon's inquisitive nature sometimes gets him into trouble, especially around stinging insects.

Stings and Bites

Bichons are forever curious and will give crawling and flying insects more attention than they deserve. This often results in potentially very harmful stings and bites around the feet or even worse around the mouth and nose.

Visible stings can be removed with a pair of tweezers. Once the sting is removed apply a saline solution or mild antiseptic. If the swelling is large, particularly inside the mouth, or if the dog appears to be in shock, consult your veterinarian at once.

Poisonous snakebites necessitate immediate action, as snake venom travels to the nerve centers very quickly. Keep the dog quiet. Venom spreads rapidly if the dog is active. Excitement, exercise, and struggling increase the rate of absorption. If possible, carry the dog. Do not wash the wound, as this increases venom absorption. Do not apply ice, as this does not slow absorption and can damage tissue. Since each snake venom requires a different antivenom, try to get a good look at the snake and describe it to your veterinarian in as much detail as you can.

Libraries often carry books that picture snakes that are commonly found in your local area. Those who live in suburban communities or in the country would be wise to familiarize themselves with what indigenous poisonous snakes look like.

Wildlife Encounters

Porcupine quills. If your Bichon's nose has come up against the porcupine's defense system and you can't get your dog to a veterinarian, do your best to muzzle the dog before attempting any relief measures. Once this is accomplished, cut the quills back to an inch or so and remove them with pliers. Pull the quills out with a straightforward motion. Your veterinarian's attention is important, even after the quills have been removed.

Skunks. If you live in the country or any area where there are skunks, my best advice is to be prepared in advance. Skunks are nocturnal creatures and no one should ever leave a Bichon to his own devices outdoors at night. However, more than one skunk has defied the nighttime rule and ventured out during the day. Your Bichon's encounter with one of these creatures can make you wish he lived in another county!

Even though a skunk encounter is not exactly a medical emergency, it requires immediate action. There are many products sold by pet shops that will eliminate the odor quickly and thoroughly. The age-old tomato juice treatment can be used, but it's not nearly effective as tradition would have us believe, and who wants a pink Bichon for the next several weeks?

Having had to deal with the problem myself, a friend's sure-fire remedy is the best I've found:

1/4 cup of baking soda
1 quart of 3 percent peroxide
1 tablespoon of "Dawn" dishwashing detergent

Spray or douse the skunking victim with the mixture and allow it to remain for approximately five to ten minutes, then wash off. Repeat the next day if necessary.

Medications

You wouldn't think the average-sized Bichon could defeat a fully grown human in the medication battle, but some of these little guys have super strength when it comes to refusing to take their medicine. A few tricks will assist you in winning the battle.

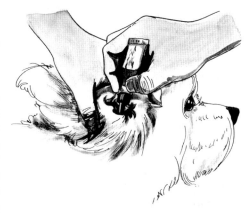

Applying ointments: Tubes with nozzle applicators allow you to aim the medication exactly where you want it to go.

Many Bichons can see medicine coming. For those dogs, it is best to hide a pill in a tasty treat. With any luck, the pill will be accepted without dispute.

Applying Ointments

Tubes with nozzle applicators help aim the medication exactly where you want it to go and can make sure it finds its intended way into the eye or down the ear canal. This type of tube also helps get ointments into punctures or cuts. Again, it is wise to muzzle your Bichon if applying an ointment that might sting or burn. The inside of a Bichon's ear is particularly sensitive and the application of medication there can sometimes be startling to your dog.

Pill Time

Although my dogs have always been able to wolf down any kind of treat the instant it gets past their teeth, they are able to detect and refuse almost anything that has a pill neatly hidden in it. Even when it gets into their mouths they are expert at eating the camouflage and ejecting the pill.

Tuna seems to work well if it is on your Bichon's top ten treats list. First give your Bichon a pill-free sample of the food to whet his appetite. Normally this insures the second treat containing the pill will go down without hesitation.

Putting medication in a dog's food dish and assuming it has been eaten is not a good idea. Many dogs have built-in pill detectors; they find a pill the size of a pinhead faster than you can say their name. These same clever detectives also know just where to hide the pill so you won't find it for a week or two!

If trickery or burying the pill in your Bichon's food doesn't work, you may have to resort to manual insertion. Do this gently and whisper sweet nothings to your dog while you do so. Simply open your dog's mouth and place the pill at the back of the tongue. Close the mouth and tilt your dog's head upwards until the pill is swallowed. To encourage swallowing, gently stroke your Bichon's throat. Once you see a "gulp" you will know the pill is on its way to doing some good. Again, some dogs are very clever about this also and have a way of swallowing without the pill's going down. So watch your patient for a few minutes afterwards to make sure the pill doesn't wind up on the floor.

Liquid Medication

Trying to put a spoonful of medicine into your Bichon's mouth can be a bigger chore than you might imagine, especially if the medicine has a taste your dog dislikes. A syringe sans needle can help you solve the problem easily.

It is best to shoot the medication into the side of the dog's mouth or under the tongue. Don't shoot any liquids directly into the throat area, as the dog could easily choke. And if you are giving a large dose, administer it slowly and make sure you give your dog time to swallow.

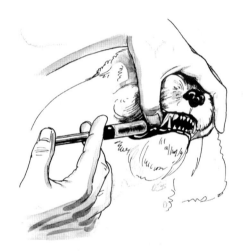

A syringe without the needle solves the problem of getting your Bichon to take his liquid medicine. Shoot the medication into the side of his mouth or under the tongue, but never directly into the throat area.

Chapter Fourteen

To Breed or Not to Breed

For many years the Bichon Frise was purebred dogdom's best kept secret. The breed was relatively well known among breeders of purebred dogs, exhibitors, and dog fanciers in general, but was rarely found in households throughout America.

And then, *and then*—the irresistibly charismatic Ch. Special Times Just Right burst into the limelight by winning Best In Show at New York's Westminster Kennel Club! The heat was on—everyone wanted a little dog "just like the one that won at Madison Square Garden."

Although popularity may sound like a good thing to the general dog lover, in the world of dog breeding, more is definitely not better! The more popular a breed becomes, the more it is apt to attract puppy mills and out-for-the-buck backyard breeders. The breed becomes a commercial endeavor and little or no attention is paid to maintaining the quality and high standards of the breed. When the "quick buck" element enters the picture nothing pos-

itive results. If anything, their arrival forecasts damage to the breed.

Today, a Bichon can be purchased from pet shops or through the classified ads in local newspapers. The ancestry of Bichons available through these outlets is questionable in respect to health and temperament. The hard work of those who have spent years keeping the breed happy and healthy is compromised.

The first thing you should do before you think further about the possibility of adding to the world's Bichon population is pay a visit to your local humane society or animal shelter. I don't know about your town, but there are thousands of purebred dogs in need of rescue all over the country—unfortunately too many of them (and even one is too many!) are Bichons.

The American Humane Society reports well over 15 million healthy and friendly dogs and cats were euthanized in the past year alone! Many of these pets were born into good homes but obviously fell into the hands of irresponsible buyers.

A litter of puppies will quickly outgrow their whelping box. By that time their mother will have washed her paws of the entire affair. From that point on the puppies will not only want to be "out," but out with you!

You may counter with the fact that you would never knowingly sell a Bichon you've bred to someone so irresponsible as to allow the dog to wind up in an animal shelter. That may be true, but once the puppy you've sold goes with its new owner and the buyer moves to some distant place, all control is lost. How can you really know what will happen to the dog or to whom that individual may give or sell the puppy you've bred?

When those fluffy little puppies start growing by leaps and bounds (none of them old enough to housebreak by the way!), getting them off to their new homes is going to be your top priority. That priority may

interfere with your making absolutely sure that the person relieving you of your burden is the right person to own a Bichon.

Pierre may well be the smartest little fellow since Lassie came home. He could also be the most devoted companion of any dog in your town and may love you beyond all reason. None of these, however, is a sound reason for being a candidate for producing offspring.

If the breeder from whom you purchased your Bichon sold the dog to you specifically as pet quality, the seller obviously had sound reasons for the dog's not being bred. You should respect the wishes and judgment of that very experienced person.

All too often I hear people who have purchased a Bichon say, "Ami needs to have a litter to complete her development" or "Pierre needs a girlfriend to relieve his frustration." Believe me, neither Ami nor Pierre needs a sexual tryst to make their lives complete. Actually, especially in the case of Pierre or any other male, breeding will serve to increase his frustration rather than relieve it.

Even if your Bichon is of the quality that warrants reproducing, there are consequences that must be considered. Ami's litter can easily bring your dog population to five or six overnight. This can be great fun for the entire family for the first three or four weeks, when the puppies spend their lives nursing and sleeping. But do mind I said, *three or four weeks.* The day arrives very quickly when Ami will look up at you as if to say, "Well, you wanted puppies—now take care of them!"

It won't be long before the puppies will outgrow not only the whelping box, but the whole room they're in! Then too, they will have transferred their dependence upon their mom to you and will want to be with you—*all the time!* Think back on the patience and work involved in housebreaking and training your single Bichon puppy. Now multiply that by four or five. Fun—I wonder!

Realize the commitment you will have to make when weaning time comes. Newly weaned puppies need four meals a day. Will you or a responsible member of the family be on hand to feed morning, noon, evening, and night?

We've talked about the need for properly socializing Bichon puppies. Not only will they object to being shunted off into the garage or the backyard, it will do nothing for their temperaments. Bichon puppies must have continuous human contact from birth on if they are to achieve their potential as companions. Ask yourself if you are willing to give them all the time they need and deserve until you have found a responsible home for each puppy in the litter. This may take weeks, sometimes months. And that's *after* you have already decided it is time for the puppies to be off to their new homes.

Some people are willing to commit to all the hard work and time involved in raising a litter of Bichons in anticipation of great financial gain. They multiply the selling price of a hypothetical number of puppies by somewhere in the area of $1,000 or more and think, "Wow, what a great source of income!"

Think again! Stop to consider the cost of a stud fee and prenatal veterinary expenses then add the cost of possible whelping problems, health checks, and the necessary inoculation series and food for the puppies. This says nothing of possibly needing veterinary help with artificial insemination. (Some inexperienced males may not know how to do the job or are simply not interested.) Caesarian sections for difficult births are not unheard of. We're talking easily of thousands of dollars here. Profit? I don't think so!

Parents who want to have their young children experience "the miracle of birth" can do so by renting videos of all kinds of animals giving birth. Handling the experience this way saves adding to pet overpopulation.

There is constant lobbying throughout America to restrict the rights of all dog owners and dog breeders because of this pet overpopulation and the unending need to destroy unwanted animals. Thoughtful dog owners will leave the breeding process to experienced individuals who have the facilities to keep resulting offspring on their premises until suitable and responsible homes can be found for them.

Who Should Breed Dogs?

Many people believe that the only real requirement for breeding dogs is just being a dog lover. I wish I could say that's true. Unfortunately, it's not. Granted, being a dog lover is an essential component of a good dog breeder's makeup. Who else would be willing to put up with all the disappointments and sheer drudgery that is often involved?

Much more is involved in becoming an accomplished breeder of dogs than loving them. In fact, a mighty long list of characteristics mirrors the one I give to people who ask me where they should buy a well-bred dog.

The responsible breeder gives every dog bred or owned all the care and attention it needs. That care even precedes the birth of the dog. Many hidden hereditary factors must be considered when mating two animals. I find it hard to believe that an irresponsible person would take the time and endure the high costs involved in determining if the breeding stock about to be used is clear of major debilitating physical problems or temperament flaws.

You must understand that no breed, no dog, no animal (human or otherwise) is entirely free of hereditary defects of some degree or another. Chapter 12 gave you a look at what can be inherited even in litters born through the efforts of those who know what they're doing.

Working with a Mentor

Breeding Bichons with the beauty and intelligence that the breed is intended to have isn't done easily. Breeding just one dog that combines *most* of what the Bichon standard requires is a genuine accomplishment. It doesn't happen by accident. If you are even thinking of breeding dogs of any kind, especially Bichons, I urge you to put yourself in the hands of an experienced and successful breeder who can guide you every step of the way. If you aren't willing to do that, you should not even think about breeding dogs!

For the first few weeks, Bichon puppies spend their lives sleeping and eating. However, as they grow, individual personalities develop and this should be considered in the homes to which they will be going.

Spaying and Neutering

Other than those purchased as show or breeding stock directly from a knowledgeable and respected breeder, all Bichons should be spayed or neutered. The procedures will not change the personality of your pet and doing so can also help avoid some of the more distasteful aspects of dog ownership.

Males that have not been altered have the natural instinct to lift their legs and urinate on objects to mark the territory in which they live. Then too, the entire male has that ongoing need to "seek and find" a girlfriend. There is no doubt he will have an even greater tendency to roam (if he stays home at all) if there is a female in heat in the area.

Females will have two estrus cycles each year that are accompanied by a bloody discharge. Unless the female is kept confined, there will be extensive soiling of the area in which she is allowed and, much more disastrous, she could become mismated and pregnant. Unspayed females also have a much higher risk of developing pyometra or mammary cancer later in life.

It is important to understand though that spaying and neutering are not reversible procedures. If you are considering the possibility of showing your Bichon, altered animals are not allowed to compete in American Kennel Club conformation dog shows. Altered dogs may, however, compete in herding and obedience trials, agility events, and field trials.

There is something very unique in the bond that can develop between well-behaved children and their dogs. They seem to have a special understanding of each other that goes beyond the world of adults.

Useful Addresses and Literature

This section lists a variety of media that you can explore as you and your Bichon investigate the many possibilities the sport of dogs offers. You'll find plenty of resources from books and magazines, videos, Web sites, and trade organizations to help you in just about any pursuit you wish to follow with your Bichon.

Kennel Clubs
American Kennel Club (AKC)
51 Madison Avenue
New York, NY 10010
Tel. (212) 696-8200
All Registration Information:
American Kennel Club
5580 Centerview Drive
Raleigh, NC 27606-3390
Tel. (919) 233-9767

Bichon Frise Club of America
Mrs. Bernice Richardson
186 Ash St. N.
Twin Falls, ID 83301

Canadian Kennel Club
89 Skyway Avenue, Unit 100
Etobicoke, Ontario
Canada M9W 6R4
Tel. (416) 675-5511 or (800) 250-8040

United Kennel Club (UKC)
100 E. Kilgore Road
Kalamazoo, Michigan 49001-5593
Tel. (616) 343-9020

Periodicals
AKC Gazette
260 Madison Avenue
New York, New York 10010
http://www.akc.org

Bichon Frise Reporter
P.O. Box 6369
San Luis Obispo, CA 93412

Bloodlines **Magazine**
United Kennel Club
100 E. Kilgore Road
Kalamazoo, Michigan 49001-5593

Dog Fancy
P.O. Box 6050
Mission Viejo, CA 92690
Tel. (800) 426-2516

Dog World
P.O. Box 6050
Mission Viejo, CA 92690
Tel. (800) 426-2516
www.dogworldmag.com

A Bichon can be a couch potato with the best of them, but he really shines in an active lifestyle. Here, a handsome Bichon sails easily over one of the jumps at an Agility trial.

Bichon Frise therapy dogs bring great happiness to hospital patients and nursing home residents everywhere. Even those who are afraid of dogs are irresistibly drawn to these endearing canine clowns.

Dogs In Canada
Apex Publishers, 89 Skyway Ave.
#200
Etobicoke, Ontario
Canada M9W-6R4

Dogs In Review
P.O. Box 6050
Mission Viejo, CA 92690
Tel. (800) 426-2516

Journal of Veterinary Medical Education
Dr. Richard B. Talbot, Editor
VA-MD College of Veterinary
Medicine
Virginia Polytechnic Institute and
State University
Blacksburg, VA 24061

Books

Stubbs, Barbara. *The Complete Bichon Frise.* New York: Howell Book House, 1990.
Beauchamp, Richard G. *Bichon Frise: A Complete Pet Owner's Manual.* Hauppage, New York: Barron's Educational Series, Inc., 1996.
_____ . *The Simple Guide to Showing Your Dog.* Neptune City, NJ: TFH Publications, Inc., 2003.
Colflesh, Linda. *Making Friends (Training Your Dog Positively).* New York: Howell Book House, 1990.
Squire, Dr. Ann. *Understanding Man's Best Friend.* New York: Macmillan Publishing Company, 1991.

Pet Travel Publications

The Automobile Association of America (AAA)
Tel. (800) 222-4357
www.aaa.com

Vacationing with Your Pet Guide
Pet-Friendly Publications
2327 Ward Road
Pocomoke City, MD 28851

Pet Travel Resources from Air Safe.com
www.airsafe.com/issues/pets.htm

Boarding Kennels and Pet Sitters

American Boarding Kennels Association
Tel. (719) 591-1113
www.abka.com

National Association of Professional Pet Sitters
1030 15th Street NW, Suite 870
Washington, DC 20005
Tel. (800) 296-7387
www.petsitters.org

Pet Sitters International
418 East King Street
King, NC 27021
Tel. (800) 268-7487
www.petsit.co

Videos

AKC and the Sport of Dogs, American Kennel Club

Right Dog for You, American Kennel Club

Breed Standard Videos, American Kennel Club

Puppies born in a well thought out breeding program vary in conformation and personality. It is extremely important that the new owner gets the puppy that will do best in the environment of the owner's household. Good breeders know the personality of each of the puppies in a litter and will do their best to create the most suitable match. Therefore it is important that the buyer gives the breeder as much information about him- or herself, their home, and their lifestyle as possible.

Web Sites

American Veterinary Medical Association	*www.avma.org*
Bichon Frise Club of America	*www. bichon.org*
Bichon Frise Rescue	*www.bichon.resq.org*
American Kennel Club	*www.akc.org*
Canadian Kennel Club	*www.ckc.ca/info*
United Kennel Club	*www.ukcdogs.com*

Identification Organizations

American Kennel Club Home Again Microchip Program
Tel. (800) 566-3596

Int. American Veterinary Identification Systems, Inc.
3179 Hammer Avenue
Norco, CA 92860
Tel. (800) 336-AVID

Poison Control

National Animal Poison Control Center
(800) 548-2423
http://www.napcc.aspca.org/

Sports and Games

North American Flyball Association, Inc.
1002 E. Samuel Avenue
Peoria Heights, IL 61614
www.flyball.org

U.S. Dog Agility Association, Inc.
P.O. Box 850955
Richardson, TX 75085-0955
www.usdaa.com

Alpo Canine Frisbee disc. Championships
Tel. (888) 444-ALPO
www.alpo.com

Therapy Dog Organizations

Therapy Dogs International, Inc.
88 Bartley Road
Flanders, NJ 07836
Tel. (973) 252-9800
tdi-dog.org/training.htm

Delta Society
289 Perimeter Road East
Renton, WA 98055-1329
Tel. (425) 226-7357
www.deltasociety.org

Index

DATE DUE

ISCTW 636
.72
B372

BEAUCHAMP, RICHARD G.
THE BICHON FRISE
HANDBOOK
6/05

ISCTW 636
.72
B372

HOUSTON PUBLIC LIBRARY
CENTRAL LIBRARY